HIP
HOTELS

CITY

HERBERT YPMA

HIP
HOTELS

with 623 illustrations, 510 in colour

AMSTERDAM

seven one seven

8

ANTWERP

de witte lelie

14

BANGKOK

the sukhothai

20

BARCELONA

hotel arts
claris hotel

24

DUBLIN

the clarence

70

FLORENCE

helvetia & bristol

76

HONG KONG

the peninsula

82

LONDON

blakes
the hempel
the metropolitan
the portobello hotel

86

NEW YORK

soho grand hotel
four seasons hotel
the mercer

160

PARIS

hôtel costes
l'hôtel
hotel lancaster
hotel montalembert

178

PORTLAND

the governor hotel

202

ROME

albergo del sole al pantheon
hotel eden
hotel locarno

208

BASEL

der teufelhof

36

BERLIN

sorat art'otel

bleibtreu

the ritz-carlton schlosshotel

42

COLOGNE

hotel im wasserturm

60

DRESDEN

schloss eckberg

64

LOS ANGELES

chateau marmont

mondrian

108

MELBOURNE

the adelphi

the prince of wales

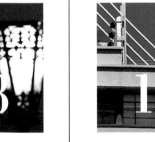

122

MIAMI

hotel astor

marlin

pelican

the tides

132

MILAN

four seasons

154

SAN FRANCISCO

hotel monaco

the phoenix

hotel rex

224

SYDNEY

regents court

240

VIENNA

das triest

244

ZURICH

widder hotel

250

introduction

In the age of 'hurry there and hurry back' the choice of hotel plays a more important role in our travel plans than ever before. As distances have become smaller, so too has the time allotted for the journey. Get into town, do as much as possible in as little time as possible: that's the mantra of the frequent flyer.

When people still made leisured journeys on lazy liners accompanied by massive steamer trunks, and trips were measured in months not hours, the choice of hotel was not of such paramount importance. There was always time to scout around for new digs if you were not enamoured with the accommodation. But now, when the journey, including getting there and getting back, lasts just days, the hotel *is* the travel experience. In the world of modern city travel, you are where you stay. And we all want to stay in a place with personality. We crave an injection of individualism to counter the soul-destroying sameness of airports, duty-free shopping centres, and airlines themselves, a sameness aptly summed up by the old Holiday Inn slogan, 'the best surprise is no surprise'.

The good news is that highly individual places do exist. *Hip Hotels: City* is devoted to them. This is a guide to hotels in the world's most interesting and frequently visited cities; to hotels that cater to that most neglected victim of twentieth-century progress – imagination. Travel, even business travel, can still be an adventure. A Hip Hotel can turn a boring business jaunt into a stylish and stimulating experience.

But much as we all want something individual, we do all have different tastes and preferences. That is why, unlike most guide books, an enormous effort was made to photograph extensively every hotel. Words, especially brochure adjectives like 'charming' and 'beautiful', mean different things to different people, and in the end mean nothing. Pictures are less ambiguous. The pictures in this book are a record of my visit to each hotel, and every photo layout is a reflection of what was worth recording. If a hotel has great bathrooms, bars, restaurants, views, food, furniture, pool, or indeed all of these, then that is what determined the choice of photographs. My goal was to capture the essence of each hotel. So now there is no excuse for an unimaginative trip.

seven one seven

Take the finest British aristocratic guest house and transplant it to the heart of one of the grooviest cities in Europe and you have Seven One Seven: an up-market, all-suite, continental inner-city version of the very best British bed and breakfast tradition.

The exterior reveals little. If it weren't for the brass plaque on the outside of this dark green, double-fronted Empire-style canal house it could easily be mistaken for the discreet residence of an old Amsterdam family. It doesn't look like a hotel on the outside, and nor does it on the inside. The 'lived-in' interior is an unexpected combination of antique and modern, African masks and classical torsos, books and walking sticks, Murano glass and cast-iron urns – exactly the kind of eclectic, unpredictable mix that might be found in an old English country house.

Some fifteen years ago Kees van der Valk, a Dutch fashion designer and decorator, came across an unforgettable bed and breakfast in Braemar, Scotland – a place where a gentleman dressed in a beautiful suit would serve high tea beside a roaring open fire in an interior of exquisite comfort and beauty. That discovery launched him on a creative mission to realize his own vision of the perfect guest house. He

toyed initially with the idea of buying a château in the French countryside, but concluded that there were already too many such converted châteaux in France and not nearly enough interesting places to stay in Amsterdam.

So the search began for the right property. In June 1996 van der Valk found the type of house that real estate people in Amsterdam will assure you 'normally never comes on the market' – a large, listed building ideally situated on the Prinsengracht, one of the main canals in the heart of the old city. After negotiating to buy the stately 1810 building back from a group of property developers intent on dividing it into eight apartments, the real work began. The Empire-style building (so called because it dates back to the brief reign of Napoleon Bonaparte's brother as King of the Netherlands) had long ago undergone a disastrous conversion into offices. A fifty-strong team set to work, stripping and virtually reconstructing the entire property. And thus in just six months it was brought back to its former domestic grandeur, and in fine style.

All plasterwork for the new ceilings was done by a team from England (Stevenson's of Norwich), and antiques were found at auctions and fleamarkets all over Europe.

Suzannah the resident Irish setter features in a reworked oil portrait by Dutch artist Bob van Blommenstein

Carefully arranged throughout the hotel are African artifacts from Tribal Art, an antique shop on nearby Spiegelstraat

Facing the courtyard to the rear, the Tolkien Suite is painted a deep, burnt tomato-red

Unusually for Amsterdam, some rooms are more the size of lofts: the Picasso Suite measures seventy square metres

This new hotel is in a double-fronted Empire house on Amsterdam's prestigious Prinsengracht

Breakfast in a hamper: a basket-full of delicious surprises is prepared for guests who cannot bear to leave their room

The stair hall revives the eighteenth-century tradition of the print room, with prints stuck directly onto the wall

Roman antiquities, African tribal art and the proprietor's own oil paintings sit on the mantelpiece of the salon fireplace

The Shakespeare Suite, a handsome, fifty-square-metre room, is elegantly decorated in tones of grey

The top-floor Picasso Suite has
an elegantly high ceiling and five
windows overlooking the canal

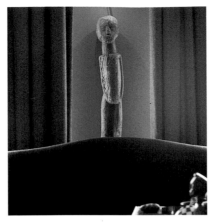

Seven One Seven is curtained
and upholstered throughout in
traditional men's suit fabrics

The Schubert Suite – a cosy, antique-
filled room with shutters, an original
beamed ceiling and a view of the canal

The Mahler Suite – English antique
oak and African photographs make
this the most popular room

Afternoon tea, included in the room
price, is served in the library, a light-
filled room stacked with design books

The Stravinsky Room is a private dining
area overlooking the courtyard – dinner
is served by prior arrangement

The quiet and secluded courtyard is
an unusual but welcome rarity for
a canal house in Amsterdam

The house number is also
the name of the hotel, situated on the
Prinsengracht – the Prince's Canal

The decoration is a personal, eclectic
mix that throws together cast-iron
urns and Murano glass

Luxurious angora-wool blankets were custom-made by the Melin Tregwynt mill in Wales; copper beds were sourced from Deptich Design in London; and architectural salvage dealers in Antwerp and Brussels supplied fireplace surrounds and other antiques. Anything that couldn't be found was commissioned from local craftsmen. Despite the rush, there was little compromise.

For Kees van der Valk it was the realization of a creative fantasy. As a graduate of the Rietveld Academy, one of Holland's top art schools, van der Valk started his career by diving enthusiastically into fashion – men's fashion. That was in the late sixties, the time of Pierre Cardin and Yves Saint Laurent, and anything was possible. Thirty years later, with the eye and attitude of a designer who has seen everything, it is perhaps not surprising that his own preference is now firmly rooted in the classic tradition of English bespoke tailoring, and so much so that the fabrics we normally associate with Savile Row – the pinstripes,

tweeds, hunting checks and houndstooth fabrics from such famous suppliers as Yorkshire-based Hunt & Winterbotham – have ended up as curtains and on chairs, couches and cushions in Seven One Seven. The wardrobe of a distinguished gentleman has become the wardrobe of a distinguished interior. Curtains are lined with raincoat fabric, partition curtains are made from Belgian twill (usually used for military uniforms), and even Suzannah, the resident Irish setter, sleeps in a basket upholstered in Harris tweed.

An impeccably turned out environment, Seven One Seven also has the very best calling card: an unbeatable location. Within easy strolling distance of the Rijksmuseum and the Van Gogh Museum, around the corner from the main antiquarian shopping street, Spiegelstraat, and within easy walking distance of all the best bars, restaurants and shops for which Amsterdam is justifiably famous, Seven One Seven is a perfect introduction to the sophisticated side of Amsterdam.

---

address Seven One Seven, Prinsengracht 717, 1017 JW Amsterdam, Netherlands

telephone (31) 20 4270 717   **fax** (31) 20 4230 717

room rates from NLG550 (suites from NLG690)

de witte lelie

Situated in the heart of Antwerp on the famous Keizerstraat, one of the city's oldest streets, this hotel has quite a pedigree. Dating back to the Flemish Golden Age, no less than three of the townhouses on the same street were once part of the life of Peter Paul Rubens. One belonged to his wealthy brother-in-law Balthazar the Great; another to Rubens' close friend, the mayor of Antwerp; and the third to another friend and colleague, the famous animal painter Frans Snyders.

This legacy of Antwerp's gilded past proved an irresistible drawcard to Monica Bock when she came across the opportunity to purchase three adjoining seventeenth-century townhouses in 1993. Inspired by all this history and charged with the idea of creating a small, intimate hotel, she and her interior designer sister, together with architect Bernard Coens, seized the challenge of combining a precious and prestigious heritage with the modernity they felt was crucial to comfort and convenience. The exclusive inner-city 'retreat' they envisaged had to be beautiful but it also had to be practical, with large bathrooms, efficient heating, up-to-date electricals, cable television and stereo – everything in fact that contemporary lifestyles demand. This meant

difficult choices had to be made on what to take away and what to keep. Resisting the temptation to divide the accommodation into a warren of little rooms, Bock decided to do the opposite: create fewer but bigger rooms. There are just ten suites in the hotel, each completely different in configuration, but all luxuriously spacious and flooded with natural light. They therefore preserve the most powerful aspect of the original interior, namely the exquisite scale of its long rectangular rooms and soaring ceilings that typify the elegant proportions of the Golden Age.

As a result the interiors of De Witte Lelie are strangely reminiscent of the world depicted in the art of the period. Staying here, it feels as if you have wandered into a painting by Vermeer. There is a clarity to this hotel's style that allows simple little canvas-covered chairs to coexist comfortably with huge baroque chandeliers. Nothing at De Witte Lelie looks out of place and nothing feels forcibly fashionable.

Its sophisticated, timeless combination of antique and modern gives De Witte Lelie a very romantic ambience. This trait of course is what distinguishes the Flemish Belgians from their Low Country Dutch neighbours.

A grand staircase, black-and-white marble floor, and lofty ceilings create the ambience of an elegant classic

Canvas-covered modern furniture from Italy contrasts effectively with antique fireplaces and old beams

Breakfast at de Witte Lelie is served in the former stables, now an elegant room overlooking the courtyard

Adjoining the breakfast room is a romantic all-white, old-world kitchen, where breakfast is prepared

All the rooms at de Witte Lelie are suites: elegant, spacious, white and comfortable

The black-and-white floor of the lobby recalls the houses portrayed by Flemish Masters

The Belgians are more sensuous; they care more about food and less about train schedules; by and large they are more concerned with comfort and luxury than with exactitude. And yet this romantic streak is tempered with a strong sense of modernity. As anyone in touch with the worlds of fashion, interior design or architecture will tell you, the Belgians can be extremely avant garde. Just look at some of Antwerp's restaurants and shops. Many people come from Germany and Holland for the weekend not just for the food but also because Antwerp has some of the most original boutiques of any European city. (The staff at De Witte Lelie can make the best, and most up-to-date, recommendations for shopping and eating in Antwerp.)

Knowing the Belgian penchant for food, I thought it strange at first that De Witte Lelie does not have its own restaurant. But given its location in the very heart of Antwerp's old city, it would be a pity not to go out and sample some of the fine choices in dining that the city can offer. De Witte Lelie does, however, have a kitchen, and it's used to prepare the breakfast (included in the room rate). And what a breakfast it is. Served in what were once the stables, a charming, light-filled, lofty space overlooking the courtyard, the whole event is superbly orchestrated by the proprietor and manager, Monica Bock. She loves this part of her day, and it shows. The entire experience feels less like staying at a hotel than being a guest at an exquisite house party.

The entrance to the breakfast room is via the spectacular all-white kitchen (also straight out of a Vermeer painting) where the aroma of freshly brewed coffee and croissants just out of the oven is only a teaser for what awaits on the table. All manner of breads, pastries, cheeses, hams, sausage and home-made jams adorn the spotless white linen, and should you want some eggs, they are cooked to your exact wishes in the cast-iron pan that is brought to your table. Thus even breakfast resembles a still-life by a Flemish Master.

---

address De Witte Lelie, Keizerstraat 16–18, 2000 Antwerp, Belgium

telephone (32) 3 226 19 66   **fax** (32) 3 234 00 19

room rates from 6,500BFr (suites from 9,000BFr)

the sukhothai

Sukhothai, or 'Dawn of Happiness', is regarded as the first true Thai kingdom. Established in 1238 in what is now north-central Thailand, it was a golden age of Thai art and civilization, a period of creativity and originality that exerted tremendous influence over subsequent periods. The kingdom itself was surprisingly short-lived, lasting only until 1376, when it became a vassal state to the city of Ayutthaya. But despite this brief lifespan it was the period of Thai history during which a national identity was forged. The Thai script was invented and Theravada Buddhism, the form practised in Thailand, was codified. It was also a period that saw the emergence of an art form – of which mainly architecture and sculpture survives – that is unique to Thailand.

In choosing the name Sukhothai, inspired by the achievements of that period of cultural flowering, this hotel gave itself a lot to live up to. Conscious of such a formidable precedent, a concentrated effort was made to evoke, in a modern sense, something of the harmony and beauty of this remote period of Thai history. To do this the hotel called on the talents of Edward Tuttle, the designer responsible for Phuket's famously idyllic retreat, the Amanpuri.

For his guiding inspiration Tuttle chose the tradition of the fabulous historic cities of Siam (as Thailand was always known before 1939). It is said that when the city of Ayutthaya was at its peak, it was one of the grandest and wealthiest cities in Asia – a thriving seaport envied not just by the Burmese but by Europeans too. The Portuguese were the first to arrive, in 1512, soon followed by the Dutch, Spanish, English and French, all of them by all accounts in great awe of the city. It was from this legacy that the Sukhothai hotel took its design cue. Set amid six acres of landscaped gardens and lily-choked reflecting pools, the sumptuous royal palaces of Siam's ancient capitals are evoked by the abundant presence of the sculpture, textures, colours and materials of Thai heritage. In the specially crafted brass lamp holders, the terracotta frames inserted into the plastered walls, the solid teak bathroom floors, the Thai silk upholstery, and particularly in the courtyard pond exhibiting replicas of thirteenth-century Sukhothai stupas, Tuttle has abstracted the most beautiful and distinctive aspects of Thai culture and reintroduced them in a manner that is elegantly pared down and unmistakably contemporary.

Tuttle's restrained teak, granite and silk have prompted some journalists to describe his design for the Sukhothai as 'Asian minimalism'. Though certainly not an inaccurate description, this still doesn't quite do the project justice. For the Sukhothai is more than an exercise in style: it is a successful attempt to project the best of Thai culture in a context where it can make a more memorable impact than in any museum. It involves the visitor to Bangkok in an extraordinarily old and refined culture which predates the Mediterranean Bronze Age by two thousand years. In fact the part of Southeast Asia we now know as Thailand was, according to world-renowned scholar Paul Benedict, the 'focal area' in the emergent cultural development of early man.

In contrast to Bangkok's recent transformation into a metropolis with some of the world's worst traffic, and in defiance of the city's conformity to the international trend for more and more high-rise towers, the Sukhothai consists of an enclave of buildings that vary in height from four to a maximum of nine storeys, all capped by simple pitched roofs. Located in the heart of Bangkok, a stone's throw from the exquisite Lumphini park, and in the centre of the lush and leafy banking and diplomatic sector, the hotel is a welcome haven from the frenetic activity of Asia's largest city. With four different restaurants (including the Celadon, one of the most authentic Thai restaurants in Bangkok, set in a traditional Thai pavilion in a water garden), six acres of flower gardens and lily ponds, a twenty-five-metre surface-tension swimming pool (its water continually spilling over the edges), a shopping arcade, beauty salon and doctor's clinic, there is no need for the jaded traveller to venture out at all. No wonder that the Sukhothai was voted the best hotel in Bangkok by *Business Traveller Magazine Asia* for three consecutive years.

In an age when we are often too rushed to absorb local colour, the design of the Sukhothai treats guests to the best of more than 750 years of Thai art and architecture.

---

address The Sukhothai, 13/3 South Sathorn Road, Bangkok 10120, Thailand

telephone (66) 2 287 02 22   **fax** (66) 2 287 49 80

room rates from US$220 (suites from US$320)

hotel arts

In the years leading up to the 1992 Olympics the entire city of Barcelona looked like a building site. If it didn't exist (a stadium or an airport, for example) it was built, and if it was looking run-down (like most of Gaudí's architectural legacy) it was renovated. Emergence from years of isolation under the iron-fisted authoritarian regime of Franco had unleashed a passion to catch up, and huge investments were being made in technology and particularly in design. The city was undergoing a massive facelift and the architects and designers responsible became the city's new celebrities. It used to be said that Barcelona was a working city, like Milan – no one would consider coming here for fun. But times have definitely changed. Things are happening here and people want to come and see for themselves. The Olympics were the spark that ignited a full-blown renaissance. A lifestyle renaissance. People now talk of *nuevo* Barcelona, and Hotel Arts may well be its most potent symbol.

There are certainly few references to Barcelona's past in the architecture of this imposing monolith designed by US architects Skidmore, Owings & Merrill. The tallest building in Barcelona, it is distinguished by a gleaming white metal framework, a scaffold-like skeleton of immense proportions that envelops the entire tower. Structurally, this protects the building from tremors and strong winds; visually, it is like a beacon that draws people to the recently rediscovered beach. Reclaimed from swamp land, the area surrounding the Hotel Arts, including the new marina, is now starting to mature into a seaside playground and yet another side to Barcelona's multi-faceted personality.

It used to be said that Barcelona lived with its back to the sea, and in pre-Olympic days it did so for good reason: the coastline was no more than a collection of derelict wharves heaped with vacant, half-dilapidated port buildings and dirty sites of heavy industry. Now the old sea wall has a far more glamorous role: it divides a four-kilometre stretch of raked sand into two public promenades packed with cafés and thronged with café society. Being next to the beach is without doubt one of the biggest attractions of Hotel Arts. Away from the traffic, noise and crowds of the city centre, adjacent to the marina, on the beach and yet still in the heart of the metropolis (ten minutes by cab), this is a hotel where you can get out of the city without having to leave it.

The lobby, furnished with pieces by Barcelona designer Pete Sans, sets the contemporary mood of the hotel

While most of this duplex suite is bright and white, the bedroom was created in sombre shades of navy blue

It seems almost impossible to build in Barcelona without reference to Gaudí, and Hotel Arts is no exception

The spectacular duplex corner apartments were originally to be sold, but are now part of the hotel

The winter garden, a light-filled lofty space, is perfect for coffee on a winter morning

Its external skeleton of white-painted steel makes Hotel Arts a distinctive Barcelona landmark

White cotton upholstery and the warmth of honey-coloured timber distinguish Tresserra's 'Casa Blanca' chair

Designed by Skidmore, Owings & Merrill, the tower's grid absorbs the energy of strong winds and tremors

The light-filled duplex apartments facing the sea were designed and furnished by Jaume Tresserra

The large windows allow an
uninterrupted view of the
sea from the bed

The tapas bar, Boyescas, features the
quixotic furniture of famed Barcelona
architect Oscar Tusquets

High-tech architecture combines
with water-filled courtyards to lend
a contemporary yet Spanish flavour

Duplex apartments on the hotel's
top floors must be the world's most
architecturally dramatic hotel rooms

Navy blue leather pieces by Jaume
Tresserra, white linens and the dark
parquet floor of a duplex bedroom

A massive fish sculpture by US architect
Frank Gehry fronts Barcelona's tallest
building and defines the beach front

Tapas, the Spanish custom of nibbling
with a drink, is the perfect introduction
to Spanish cuisine

The all-marble bathrooms are open-
plan, allowing spectacular views of
the city or ocean from the bath

Overlooking a water-filled internal
courtyard, the fitness centre
takes up two floors

In an area that less than a decade ago was marshland, people now play beach volleyball, eat in beachside cafés, stroll around the massive marina complex admiring all the swanky yachts, and generally indulge in a seaside experience that, in Franco's day, was only to be had by driving out of the city and either heading north to the Costa Brava or south to the Costa del Sol.

In addition to the distinctly hedonistic attraction of its location, the towering size of Hotel Arts also introduces the benefit of scale. Rising a majestic 153 metres above the sea, the hotel offers 455 rooms and extraordinary facilities. This is the first European property for the Ritz Carlton group, and they didn't skimp on anything. There is a large, beautiful swimming pool with its own private deck overlooking the sea, a two-storey gym of a size more often found in Manhattan than Europe, and of course spectacular views over the Mediterranean, the marina and the city from most rooms. Yet despite all the mod cons there

is never any mistaking that you are in Barcelona. Throughout the hotel, furniture by some of Spain's most gifted designers is featured alongside a substantial collection of contemporary Spanish art (hence the hotel's name) including artists Miguel Rasero, Xavier Grau and Mateo Vilagrasa. The hotel's tapas bar Goyescas, for example, features the highly distinctive furniture of architect Oscar Tusquets, a one-time collaborator and protégé of Salvador Dalí. As a result, the atmosphere could not be more evocative of Barcelona. By investing in art, architecture and design, the Ritz Carlton group has created a distinctive style and ambience. No wonder *Tatler* magazine voted it hotel of the year in 1997.

People still compare Barcelona to Milan – because it is still an important industrial centre – but with its new-found *joie de vivre*, they also now compare it to Naples. Perhaps this is why, despite its size, the Hotel Arts is almost always booked to capacity. Everyone, it seems, would rather be by the beach.

address Hotel Arts, Carrer de la Marina 19–21, 08005 Barcelona, Spain

telephone (34) 93 221 10 00 **fax** (34) 93 221 10 70

room rates from 45,000ptas (suites from 60,000ptas)

claris hotel

While some hotels possess enough art treasures and antiques to merit the description 'museum-like', it's not often that a hotel *is* a museum. Claris Hotel is the exception. Described by *Vogue* as 'the most chic hotel in Barcelona', this, surely, must be the only hotel in the world with its own museum of Egyptology, not to mention a lobby decorated with genuine Roman marble busts and fragments of mosaic floors two millennia old.

In most countries such antiquities would be firmly under lock and key, pride of place in a fortress-like museum, not casually scattered about a hotel lobby. But guests at Claris Hotel are surrounded by 4,000-year-old Egyptian masks and 2,000-year-old Roman relics. And not just in the lobby: all the guest rooms feature rare objets d'art in the form of framed sketches from nineteenth-century Egyptian archaeological excavations; thirteenth- and fourteenth-century Hindu stone sculptures; English Victorian antiques; and old Turkish kilims covering the parquet floors. Marble bathrooms, purple bedspreads and examples of modern Spanish design complete an eccentric design scheme that certainly has little in common with your run-of-the-mill hotel room.

But the absolute *pièce de résistance* of Claris Hotel is the mezzanine museum of Egyptology. Here, one of the world's finest private collections of ancient mummies, statues, carvings and decorated tombs is arranged purely for the interest and enjoyment of the hotel guests. There are no burly security guards keeping check, nor is the atmosphere so rarefied that you can't wait to leave. In fact, guests are encouraged to use this exotic space to take afternoon tea. There, surrounded by pieces large and small created during the zenith of Egyptian civilization, it's possible for a little while to indulge the most escapist of Indiana Jones fantasies.

This vast collection of priceless antiquities is no marketing gimmick. Rather, it is the passion of Señor Jordi Clos i Llombart, a leading member of one of Barcelona's oldest families and one of Spain's foremost Egyptologists. The hotel's museum contains only part of a continually expanding private collection that was once housed in his family home. Now even the hotel's museum, lobby spaces and all 120 rooms are not space enough, and the remaining pieces reside in Barcelona's Egyptology Museum, an institution also established and funded by Señor Clos.

Any other hotel blessed with such a priceless collection of ancient artifacts would probably opt for a conservative, stately design. Señor Clos, however, was not interested in playing safe. Employing the services of Olympic-village architects Martorell, Bohigas & Mackay resulted in architecture as visually challenging as the Roman busts, Hindu stone sculptures, kilim rugs and English Victorian antiques it frames. Strictly speaking, these pieces should not go together, yet somehow they work in an environment where the design is allowed – encouraged, even – to compete with them. It's an approach that is very much in keeping with Barcelona's unique decorative and architectural heritage. 'Modern' in this city is not modern as we know it. Do not expect pared-down, simple interiors. Rich colours; intricately patterned stone and marble; curved, organically shaped furniture in exotic woods – these are the ingredients of Barcelona's 'modern', and so too of Claris Hotel. But perhaps Señor Clos sums it up best when he describes the hotel as 'an act of romanticism … a small outburst of stone amongst so much cement'.

Like most good museums and all the best hotels, the Claris is blessed with a great location. Staying here, the metropolitan heart of Barcelona is literally at your doorstep. Claris Hotel is only one street away from the famous Paseo de Gracia, a graceful avenue paved in tiles originally designed by Gaudí that is probably the most stylish thoroughfare in Barcelona. Broad, tree-lined and packed with exclusive shops, it leads all the way to Las Ramblas, prompting *Vogue* to brand it 'a street that offers maximum expenditure for minimum effort'. Without much planning or a map, it is very easy from Claris Hotel to get out and discover the real Barcelona. But don't dress down: Barcelonans are very style-conscious. Where else in the world would you see people on scooters wearing suede riding helmets and quilted hunting coats over their impeccably tailored grey tweed suits and suede brogues?

address Claris Hotel, Pau Claris 150, 08009 Barcelona, Spain
telephone (34) 93 487 62 62   **fax** (34) 93 215 79 70
room rates from 22,000ptas (suites from 40,000ptas)

der teufelhof

Der Teufelhof is a funky art hotel amid the chimneys and factories of Switzerland's pharmaceutical city. 'Teufelhof' literally means 'the house of the devil', and in this case the devil has a very fine house indeed, complete with two theatres, a fine restaurant, a bar, a café, a brasserie (the Weinstube), an underground archaeological museum, a subterranean wine shop and accommodation for guests in both an 'Art' Hotel and a 'Gallery' Hotel (read on to discover the difference). Quite a complex really, even for a devil.

How it got here is a great story. The proprietors, Monica and Dominique Thommy Kneschaurek, both seasoned actors, had been touring Europe with a specially designed mobile theatre for seven years. Tired of travel and looking to settle, they returned to Dominique's birthplace, Basel, with an idea to combine food and theatre. Their creation, a café-theatre, was a great success, and it quickly became a part of Basel's cultural landscape. So successful was it in fact that they were eventually forced to look for a larger space. Thus they came across an abandoned house in a state of ruin on Leonhardsgraben, a pleasant street in the old part of town. But the local residents were not sympathetic to

their plans to restore some dignity to the stately old building. Basel, the residents argued, didn't need another restaurant, or bar, or theatre, or small hotel … and as a result the next *six* years were spent in a letter-writing paper war in an effort to win planning permission. Eventually, they wore down the residents' resolve and as a monument to their struggle one wall of the upstairs theatre has been papered with just a small sample of this correspondence hell.

The original idea for the concept of the hotel came from friends in the art world. The Thommys were determined to create an environment in which people could experience art in a new and more immediate way than is ever possible in a gallery or studio. Each room was therefore furnished in a simple, modern style to provide a 'blank canvas' for artists, who were then invited to use the space to create an installation. The result is not simply art as decoration, but art as an interactive experience. Examples include sound-sensitive light installations that respond to different sounds with different coloured lights, or phosphorescent painted lines that seem to float in the dark. The occupant of the room lives with and becomes part of the art installation.

Bathrooms are white, bright and
minimal – appropriately neutral
for an art-minded hotel

The restaurant, Bel Etage, awarded a
Michelin star, features a cemented-in
library as an installation piece

The Gallery Hotel has floors of African
Wenge wood and furniture by
Achille Castiglioni

Der Teufelhof has two theatres – the black and white graphic depicts the plays that have been shown so far

In the Art Hotel, rooms are large, white and empty – a deliberately blank canvas for the art installation

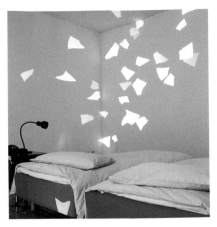

Brigitte Kordina from Vienna created this wall projection complete with soundtrack that simulates falling glass

And in an effort to stay fresh and give as many artists as possible an opportunity to participate, the rooms of the Teufelhof Art Hotel change at least once every three years.

The Thommys' formula of mixing art, theatre and food has proved an unprecedented success. The restaurant, Bel Etage, under chef Michael Baader, has earned a Michelin star; the theatre plays to a consistently full house; and the art installation rooms are so much in demand that they are booked far in advance. Thus when the building next door became available, Monica and Dominique did not hesitate to expand. The latest addition is the Gallery Hotel. Here all twenty-four rooms simultaneously exhibit the work of a single artist, with the twist that all of it is for sale, just as it would be in a commercial art gallery. The artist exhibited throughout the Gallery Hotel changes every year. Living with the art, Dominique explains, is a different kind of interaction, in a less pretentious, more relaxed environment than a gallery.

In decor, as with the Art Hotel, the rooms of the Gallery Hotel were approached with a sense of neutral simplicity, although for the newer hotel the design quotient was upped. All of the rooms have immaculate, gleaming parquet floors of dark Wenge timber, while bathrooms are paved in a typically Italian terrazzo. Half the rooms are furnished with pieces by the renowned Swiss designer Kurt Thut. The other half contain modern classics by legendary Italian designers Vico Magistretti and Achille Castiglioni. For fans of classic modern Italian furniture, the Gallery Hotel is paradise.

I was very curious, I admit, given the avant-garde nature of Der Teufelhof and the not insignificant size of the entire enterprise, to discover who, besides me, stays here? The answer is surprising. Apparently many visiting executives (who come to Basel for the pharmaceutical industry) prefer this to a 'boring' business hotel. And why not? To wear a suit is not necessarily to lack imagination.

---

address Der Teufelhof, Leonhardsgraben 47–49, CH–4051 Basel, Switzerland

telephone (41) 61 261 10 10 **fax** (41) 61 261 10 04

room rates from 155SFr (suites from 385SFr)

Die Bibliothek

sorat art'otel

Berlin is unlike any other city in Germany. While its western half was stranded like an island for almost three decades, its eastern portion was hidden away from the world behind an impregnable wall. West Berlin developed a fast-living, pressure-cooker mentality, while East Berlin was pickled by its repressive regime. This is a unique experience – no other city in the world has ever been subjected to such extreme circumstances – and as a result the now-reunited Berlin has developed a unique personality.

Until the Wall came down in 1989, an event most Germans did not believe they would see in their lifetime, few seriously wondered how these two halves would get along. There has been some tension, admittedly, but the unification has generally proceeded smoothly and has surely left Berlin one of the most interesting cities in the world to visit. The fast-paced mentality of West Berlin, which has always attracted a large youth contingent (creating a vivacious night life that's among the best in Europe), is now combined with the intriguing austerity of its eastern counterpart, an area that despite the reunification of the city and country is still vastly different from West Berlin, and is certainly still an eye-opener to

anyone who has never before ventured behind the former Iron Curtain. Here is an opportunity to see at first hand how different regimes moulded the same people in a completely different way, like twins separated at birth and raised in totally different circumstances. It's fascinating to be able once again to see the historic civic buildings, churches and grand museums that the Communists hid from the West, and to experience the oddly haunting totalitarian architecture – the impossibly broad avenues and the endless blocks of identical modern buildings – erected for the citizens of the former German Democratic Republic.

Berlin is now the largest construction site in the world, an unbelievable thicket of towering cranes, heavy machinery and scaffolding. This intense activity only heightens the sense that this, indeed, is a city where things are happening. It's no surprise then that the Sorat Art'otel was one of the first of its kind to open anywhere in the world. Berlin has always been the melting-pot of central Europe. For the past three hundred years immigrants from the far corners of Europe, including Poles, Bohemians and French Huguenots, have been drawn to this city and they have played a major role in the development of the Berlin character.

Tolerant and vivacious with a sardonic sense of humour, this is a character naturally predisposed and open to art – especially, in Berlin's case, avant-garde art.

The premise of the Art'otel is simple: surround the guests with modern art in order to create an entirely new hotel experience. In the case of the Sorat Art'otel (there are two others, one in Potsdam and one in the Nicolai quarter of former East Berlin), Austrian architects Johanne and Gernot Nalbach used a collection of works by artist Wolf Vostell as the creative point of departure. He was allowed as much latitude as was practically possible to create a different environment. Original graphics, sculptures and installations by Vostell (best known for his sculpture of two Cadillacs cemented into a public square in Berlin) adorn each and every room as well as the hotel's public areas. But perhaps more than just art itself, the hotel is distinguished by an 'artistic attitude'. In every possible detail, the interior expresses a distinctive avant-garde signature. With the carpet in the dining room designed by David Hockney, the toilets designed by Philippe Starck, or the Javier Mariscal stools at the reception desk which doubles as an espresso bar, the hotel consistently avoids convention. The outcome of this approach of invention and creativity is a very relaxed atmosphere, and a hotel that is fun because it doesn't take itself too seriously. Traditional Germanic formality is nowhere to be found.

Perhaps most impressive is that all this comes at affordable rates. This is not an elite hotel. Despite its much sought-after position (just off the Kurfürstendamm, not far from Zoo Station) the prices are nowhere near as exclusive as the locale. As a result the youthful approach is complemented by a youthful clientele. The crowd breakfasting in the morning could be a scene out of any fashionable café. The atmosphere is relaxed, the uniform generally black (tight black), and the scene seductively artistic.

address Sorat Art'otel, Joachimstaler Strasse 29, D–10719 Berlin, Germany
telephone (49) 30 88 44 70 **fax** (49) 30 88 44 77 00
room rates from DM235 (doubles from DM275)

bleibtreu

A young hotel on an old street, Bleibtreu is a streetwise hangout behind the gentlemanly guise of a city townhouse. Situated on Bleibtreu Strasse, a famous little stretch of expensive boutiques just off the Ku'damm (the Kurfürstendamm, Berlin's great shopping boulevard), it's a welcome addition. Now, finally, the chic shoppers of Berlin have somewhere to go for lunch or a quick cappuccino. The only problem is that no one, taxi drivers included, seems to know that this is a hotel. Admittedly it's a brilliant disguise. From the street the Bleibtreu is a deli, a café and a flower shop, with a bar (the Blue Bar) and a restaurant (the 31) directly behind the café. The hotel part of the equation is subtle, very subtle. Between the café and the trendy florist there is an archway over a diagonal path leading into a blue-pebbled courtyard. Situated beneath a beautiful old chestnut tree, the courtyard looks out over the restaurant and then leads back inside to a small desk tucked into a corner. This is the front desk, the reception desk … in fact the only desk.

In deciding to be different, Bleibtreu has blown away all hotel conventions, including the lobby and the reception desk. Why waste space, they say, on chairs that people never sit in and tables that spend most of the day supporting fresh flower arrangements? They have a point. Why waste the space when it can be used for fun things like cafés, bars, delis and restaurants? This way the hotel becomes a real part of the city, a participant in everyday life. And for the guests it makes a refreshing change. Instead of asking the concierge (which they don't have anyway) for suggestions on the city's latest and greatest, you can simply hang out here, secure in the knowledge that you're not missing out, because this is the place where it's all happening.

But it's not just in the public spaces that Bleibtreu has decided to be different. The rooms also follow a new spirit perhaps best described as an eco-based design logic. A desire for calm and healthy well-being underpins the fine detail and the overall concept of this hotel alike. Special organic porous paints allow the walls to breathe, all carpets are one hundred per cent virgin wool and the furniture is of untreated oak. Toxic chemicals are as much pared down as the interior aesthetic. But does that mean the place looks like a collection of hospital rooms? Far from it. The overall impression created by this eco-friendly approach is a kind of soft, new-age modernism.

Natural timber, natural colour
and organic paint express Bleibtreu's
eco-sensitive approach to design

Each floor of Berlin's Hotel Bleibtreu
is colour-coded: yellow and white
define the second floor

Timney-Fowler's neoclassically
inspired fabrics are combined
with fifties furniture

With a manager who used to be
a chef, food is taken very seriously
at Hotel Bleibtreu

An off-the-wall wall-clock is the
only decoration in the ground-floor
reception area

The Blue Bar is a popular little
pre-dinner haunt adjacent to
the ground-floor café

Even room numbers are done
differently – as illuminated
portholes set into the wall

Cotton sheets, hypo-allergenic wool
carpet, linen and cotton upholstery, and
an apple instead of a chocolate

Dressed in the style of a neoclassical
tented pavilion, the top-floor rooms
make the most of attic spaces

The delicatessen (along with a café and a flower shop) is one of the unconventional lobby tenants

The crisp, shiny terrazzo floors of the stair hall are made of glass chunks set in polished cement

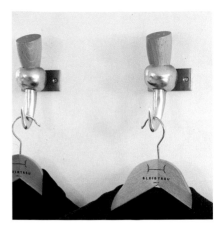

Modern, organic, funky, different: this is how best to describe Bleibtreu

Each floor has a different colour scheme: the top floor is black, white and red

The café, where guests and locals drop in for a quick cappuccino and croissant, has great ambience

The ground-floor flower shop is as much an attraction for locals as for hotel guests

Taking up most of the ground floor, the restaurant has a view over two different courtyards

Some of the sun-drenched top-floor rooms facing Bleibtreu Strasse feature small terraces

The ground-floor courtyard makes the hotel entrance an unusual outdoor-indoor-outdoor experience

It reminds me, for some reason, of California – of the interior of a 'fifties' beach house on the Pacific coast. The rooms are bright, clear and gentle, with nothing aggressive about them, nothing hard-edged. Being here inspires you to eat fruit and practise yoga … and then ruin it all by misbehaving in the bar and restaurant downstairs.

All of the accessories, furniture, carpets and lamps were specially designed for Bleibtreu by Herbert Jakob Weinand and made by hand in Germany and Italy. But perhaps the most unusual and attractive feature of the design is the lighting – and not just the lamps themselves but the manner in which they are controlled. All the lights – bedside, ceiling halogens, bathroom, make-up mirror and ambient – can be not only dimmed, but dimmed independently of each other. Once the desired mood is reached, they can be set and the levels recorded. All the adjustment and programming is done with a special remote control which (thankfully) the staff explain

how to use. Press a button and the lighting level you prefer is recalled from memory. Now that's what I call a smart room.

Even the gym did not escape Weinand's comprehensive vision. In fact it's not a gym, it's a 'wellness centre'. This is not a place where you exert yourself, but a place where other people exert themselves to help you, the guest, relax. The greatest effort required of you is that of opening the door to the sparkling steam room and lowering yourself into the dipping pool. Situated in the basement of the building, the spa space is one of the most beautiful I've seen. There is also a massage centre with a full-time holistic masseur and, most intriguingly, a special post-steam relaxing area that uses coloured lighting to help stimulate a particular mood (red light for people going out, blue light for those having an early night). If it all sounds very different, that's because it is.

And what, ultimately, is the point of all this eco-friendly concern for your well-being? The answer is elementary – a good night's sleep.

---

address Bleibtreu, Bleibtreustrasse 31, D–10707 Berlin, Germany

telephone (49) 30 884 74 0 **fax** (49) 30 884 74 444

room rates from DM275 (suites from DM525)

the ritz-carlton schlosshotel

Even the bathroom slippers feature the insignia 'Designed by Karl Lagerfeld'. It appears on everything from the matches to the complimentary bathroom cosmetics. The point that the Ritz-Carlton Schlosshotel is making is that this is no ordinary hotel. And clearly it isn't. Even without the input of Germany's most famous name in fashion, this palace, in the exclusive Grunewald area of Berlin, would be impressive enough. Originally built for Walter von Pannwitz, an aristocratic lawyer with a passion for Meissen porcelain, law reform and Dutch Masters, it was, from the day it was completed in 1914, one of the most extraordinary residences in Berlin. Kaiser Wilhelm II was entertained here on a regular basis throughout the war, as were many of Europe's reigning royals. Berlin in the early twentieth century was the fastest growing and most vibrant capital not just of recently unified Germany but of all of Europe, and Palace Pannwitz quickly became the most exclusive address in Grunewald, the city's finest neighbourhood.

Grunewald (literally 'green forest') was an area developed from the royal hunting forests that surrounded the old Prussian city. Careful planning (including the creation of a series of lakes) and strict zoning that permitted only one house per two hectares of land ensured that Grunewald, intended as an exclusive residential area, would stay that way. And it has. Conveniently located at the beginning of the Kurfürstendamm, Berlin's super sophisticated shopping strip, Grunewald today is still a forest. As Karl Lagerfeld exclaims in the hotel video, 'where else in the world can you stay in a palace, in a forest, in the middle of the city?'

The German recession following the devastation of World War I brought an end to the high life in Grunewald, and the Pannwitz family, despite having built the house as the ultimate expression of their passion for art, architecture and design, were forced to follow Kaiser Wilhelm into exile in Holland. The house was never a home again. Schloss Pannwitz remained closed and shuttered for the better part of a decade and after wartime use (first as the Croatian embassy and then as British Army HQ) it was finally converted to a hotel during Germany's Reconstruction period.

Today, because of Lagerfeld's involvement, the old palace is probably closer to its original design than at any time since World War I. Rather than impress upon it his personal stamp, Lagerfeld chose to defer to history.

Kaiser Wilhelm II was a frequent guest in the days when the Ritz-Carlton Schlosshotel was a private villa

The Kaiser Suite has all the sumptuous grandeur of a Prussian prince's boudoir

Suitably formal and impossibly grand, the Vivaldi restaurant offers one of the finest dining experiences in Berlin

A chic lobby where guests can sit
down when they check in
– how civilized!

Karl Lagerfeld's own suite is in the
cultivated and affluent Geheimrat
architectural style

Lagerfeld's suite, available if he is not in
residence, features the work of avant-
garde French designer André Dubreuil

A team of talented craftsmen from Poland was brought in to restore the gilded panelling, the massive doors and the ornate detailing that originally embellished the grand spaces of Herr von Pannwitz's house. Other craftsmen set about the task of renovating the hotel's numerous paintings and its substantial collection of antiques. The result speaks for itself. The Ritz-Carlton Schlosshotel offers not just the opportunity to stay in a palace in a forest in the city, but also an opportunity to experience a style and architecture that these days only exists in coffee-table books and heritage houses. Where else can you dine in a room originally designed to entertain a Kaiser and a Tsar? Or lunch in a winter garden intended for afternoon teas with the Dutch and Danish royal families? But part of the fun is the fact that all this happens right in the centre of the city, meaning you can indulge in a sumptuous lunch, a stroll through the forest, and some serious shopping ... all in the same afternoon.

Lagerfeld, however, did get an opportunity to put his personal stamp on one part of the hotel. In consideration of his involvement he was given an apartment within the old palace – the original private apartment in fact of Walter von Pannwitz. This was his opportunity to impart an individual signature. The suite, comprising a small entrance hall, a generously proportioned sitting room with views of the garden, and an equally large bedroom, was redecorated in a style that is rich without being fussy; elegant, but not too dainty or refined. Lagerfeld created this style by introducing select antiques and works by his favourite avant-garde designer André Dubreuil and the architect Borek Sipek. When the apartment is not in use (which, owing to his schedule, and all his other houses, is most of the year) it's available for hotel guests as an alternative to the other suites. Just for the bathroom alone it's probably worth it, not to mention the cachet of being able to say 'oh yes, we just spent the weekend in Karl's place in Berlin'.

---

address The Ritz-Carlton Schlosshotel, Brahmsstrasse 10, D–14193 Berlin, Germany

telephone (49) 30 895 84 0   **fax** (49) 30 895 84 800

room rates from DM555 (suites from DM950)

hotel im wasserturm

A decade ago, Andrée Putman was the most sought-after designer in the world. The style that she created for herself in a loft space in Paris was the catalyst for a seemingly never-ending series of prestigious design commissions.

Spare, elegant and unmistakably French, the sense of style Putman introduced was one prevalent in Paris just before World War II. It is very similar in spirit to the work of legendary designer Jean-Michel Frank. Svelte, disciplined and entirely free of frippery – no knick knacks, no cushions, no frilly fabrics, no chintz curtains – Putman's creations were not so much design as a visual extension of who she was. Design and designer were one and the same. She was already well known to an inner circle of Paris cognoscenti, but after completing the design of Morgan's Hotel in Manhattan she became an international star.

Nobody had seen anything like it. The rooms followed Putman's pared-down preference, rooted in the concept that 'modernity is best glimpsed through dramatic understatement'. The bathrooms, for example, adventurously tiled in black and white with self-standing, unadorned stainless-steel sinks, were among the most photographed spaces of the early eighties. New York had its first cool

hotel. Instead of catering to people's tastes, people had to adjust their tastes to the hotel. And it worked. Morgan's enjoyed among the highest occupancy rates in New York and for Putman it was the stepping stone to bigger and better things. She launched her own furniture company, Ecart International, manufacturing lamps originally designed by Venetian legend Mariano Fortuny and furniture by then-forgotten architect Eileen Gray, and she was commissioned to work on a uniquely innovative and daring architectural metamorphosis: the conversion of a nineteenth-century water tower, the largest of its kind in Europe, into a luxury hotel.

This was a dream job. Not only was the tower round – her favourite shape – but the sheer scale of the building promised extraordinary proportions. And there was the plus that the consortium commissioning the hotel had a reputation for insisting on quality. Where perhaps a lot of her work in New York was compromised by budget restraint (maximum effect for minimum cash) this consortium took a typically German long-term view and went for quality. The doorknobs, the furniture, the lighting, the fabrics, the bathrooms: every carefully considered aesthetic detail came off the drawing boards of her design company. The result, completed in 1990, is one of the most original and refined hotel design experiences in Europe.

And for once, the best rooms are not the most expensive. Situated on the sixth floor, these studio rooms are reached via a high-tech steel bridge suspended within the hollow core of this gigantic brick structure. The space, entered through imposingly tall doors of African Wenge wood, is divided into two rooms: a living area/study and a bedroom with en suite bathroom. With impossibly high ceilings and a pristine white tiled floor, it's the kind of space I would love to have as an apartment. It's all anyone would need, a splendid lesson in the importance of scale and space (quality) versus size (quantity). With their round walls, elegantly tall windows and timeless velvet-upholstered furniture inspired by Putman's trademark love of the thirties, these rooms are an inspiration for the potential of space given the right approach.

Anyone with an eye for interior design and architecture could lose themselves for hours in the extraordinary attention to detail. But there's more. Especially in the summer months the Wasserturm also happens to be one of Cologne's most popular restaurants. Situated on the roof and built (inevitably) in the round, this glass-enclosed space, with its myriad of sliding doors, opens out on to a terrace with a panoramic vista of Cologne. The view takes in the famous cathedral, the Rhine and the old medieval city built alongside. Here Putman abandoned her pared-down signature and recreated instead the style of a typical bourgeois Parisian restaurant, complete with comfortable reproduction Louis XV chairs, large round tables and crisp linen tablecloths. This struck me as an odd design choice given her penchant for spareness and simplicity. But then I remembered an interview in which Putman was asked her definition of good taste. She replied that she distrusted perfection – 'I always look for the mistake'.

address   Hotel im Wasserturm, Kaygasse 2, 50676 Cologne, Germany

telephone (49) 221 200 80   **fax** (49) 221 200 88 88

room rates from DM320 (suites from DM440)

schloss eckberg

Known as the 'Baroque Florence', Dresden was Germany's most beautiful large city until World War II. Transformed in the 1700s from a perennial 'also-ran' to nearby Meissen, famed for its porcelain, Dresden came into its own under the staunch but ruthless rule of Emperor Augustus the Strong, who gathered around him a brilliant group of artists and architects and turned the city into a masterpiece of Baroque architecture. Dresden replaced Meissen as the cultural and political capital of Saxony and became one of Europe's leading centres of the performing arts, a position it is reclaiming today. The city survived World War II largely unscathed until the nights of 13 and 14 February 1945, when it endured one of the most savage saturation bombing campaigns inflicted on any European city during the war. Most of Dresden's Baroque treasures were flattened and, to add insult to injury, the city shortly thereafter fell under the stifling blanket of Communist rule, disappearing from Western view behind the Iron Curtain until German reunification in 1990.

Today things are much changed. It is widely agreed that Dresden has adapted better to the economic framework of reunited Germany than any other former East German city. Like Berlin it's an exciting place to be because there is so much happening. Ironically enough, Dresden under the GDR was known as the 'land of the clueless' because its hilly topography made it one of the few places in East Germany unable to receive West German television. Perhaps this isolation was no bad thing. Most of the spectacular buildings unharmed by the Allied bombing raids have stood untouched since the war simply because there was no use for them in an egalitarian society. Now inner-city Dresden is restoring the most striking remnants of its Baroque heritage. The Semper Oper (the opera house, named after architect Gottfried Semper) is once again a prominent venue in the world of classical music. Dresden, where Wagner premiered *The Flying Dutchman* and Richard Strauss debuted *Salome*, is making a comeback as one of the world's great cultural centres.

Many Berliners head here for weekends, and arriving in the city by boat it's easy to understand why. Picturesque hilly country descends steeply to the sparkling Elbe, with castle after castle perched on vineyard-clad river banks. This is the Germany of Wagnerian legend, where blonde sirens with braided pigtails are out picking grapes in the sun.

A nineteenth-century Gothic folly
on a grand scale, Schloss Eckberg was
recently restored to its original glory

Gilded tent ceilings and uniquely shaped
pagoda doors typify the style Dresden
developed as capital of Saxony

With views over the hotel's private
park and the River Elbe, the café
is an idyllic setting for breakfast

One of the suites features its own adjoining Gothic library and picturesque views over the river

The monumental scale and ornate detailing have not been overwhelmed by an excess of decoration

In contrast to the neo-Gothic style of the villa, the bathrooms are thoroughly modern creations in marble and stone

Understandably, tourism is one of the city's growing industries. One of the palaces built by Augustus the Strong has been converted into a very plush hotel, the Taschenberg Palais, and there is even a very avant-garde hotel filled with the latest design innovations from Italy. But in a sense these places do not capture the unique prospect of this city. To experience the Dresden of legend you have to be perched in a castle above the river, where, from your room in a tower, you can watch the boats winding their way along one of Europe's most beautiful rivers. This is the magic of Schloss Eckberg. A rambling, asymmetrical Gothic folly inspired by Tudor-style estates in England and Scotland, it comes complete with its own thirty-five-acre park, a commanding perch on the River Elbe, and its own vineyard clinging to the banks of the river. Designed in 1859 by Christian Friedrich Arnoldt, a student of Gottfried Semper, its myriad of towers and bays couldn't be more suited to its picturesque position on a tree-covered rocky slope.

Expropriated by the East German government after World War II, the castle was returned to its owners shortly after reunification. During the Communist decades it had been used for little more than the odd union meeting. Thus when the new owners asked Italian architect Danili Silvestrin to redesign the interiors in a contemporary but faithful manner, the original architecture was still largely intact. Today it houses a series of highly individual and unmistakably modern interiors. Sensitive to the original spaces created by the towers and bays, the pared-down interior provides an effective counterpoint to the more fanciful architecture. White walls and modern furniture combined with the odd Biedermeier antique only accentuate the view of the Elbe and Dresden's *Altstadt*. From one of the exquisite tower suites, it's easy to understand why this area is referred to as 'the Switzerland of Saxony' and why Dresden is once again one of the great artistic capitals of Europe.

address   Schloss Eckberg, Bautzner Strasse 134, 01099 Dresden, Germany
telephone (49) 351 8099 0   **fax** (49) 351 8099 199
room rates from DM380 (suites from DM600)

the clarence

The Clarence is not a new hotel. It has been part of the Dublin scene since 1852, when it was first built as a railway hotel for out-of-towners. Located in the heart of Dublin's Temple Bar district, on the banks of the River Liffey, the hotel, by virtue of its architectural integrity and its prime location, has always managed to retain dignity and charm, even when it was well beyond its prime. It was this faded charm that endeared the hotel to the artists, musicians and writers who began to make Temple Bar the happening area in Dublin in the seventies. Among the regulars enjoying a pint at the Clarence in those days were members of the band U2. Fond memories of the place prompted Bono and the Edge to join a consortium of Irish investors to purchase the hotel with a view to restoring it.

As one American journalist observed, 'rock stars used to trash hotels, now they own them'. But of course rock stars, if anyone, should know a thing or two about hotels, since they live in them for months on end when on tour. The Clarence renovation, accordingly, was determined to a great extent by U2's own vision of their ideal place to stay. They wanted an intimate hotel, with great service, in the tradition of Irish hospitality, yet not stuffy and

definitely contemporary in its design direction. To realize their vision they employed some of the best people in the industry. Paris-based Grace Leo-Andrieu, advising manager of Hotel Montalembert and proprietor of the recently renovated Hotel Lancaster (also Hip Hotels), was brought in as consultant, and Keith Hobbs (a former associate of Terence Conran) of London-based United Designers was given responsibility for design.

And design is what sets the Clarence apart. In the early 1900s the hotel was renovated in the Arts and Crafts style, with distinctive, sober panelling in Irish oak, practical leather chairs and the occasional flourish of terrazzo floors. This 'oak and leather' came to distinguish the Clarence in the memories of several generations of regulars, and it was therefore decided that the Arts and Crafts style should also form the basis of the new interior. Hence the new Clarence is defined from top to toe, from the public spaces to the fifty guest rooms, by a subtle palette of Portland stone and American oak, and by the rich colours (cardinal red, royal blue and gold) of its leather-upholstered chairs, sofas and benches. *Condé Nast Traveler* magazine described this style as 'understated – in a context of unstinting luxury'.

The Tea Room, the Clarence's award-winning restaurant, features traditional Irish dishes with a continental twist

The 'Study', in the Arts and Crafts style, is a quiet and relaxed place to enjoy a continental breakfast or evening drink

A substantial collection of original works by Irish artist Guggi is dispersed throughout the hotel

The Clarence's all-white tiled
bathrooms continue the Arts and
Crafts style of the ground floor

The lobby is a warm and inviting place
with original Irish oak panelling
installed at the turn of the century

Rooms are calm and comfortable,
with Egyptian cotton sheets, solid oak
furniture and white Portland stone

It's a style that makes the Clarence a very comfortable place to stay, yet without making it too precious. As Harry Crosbie, one of the founding entrepreneurs, explains: 'the hotel couldn't be too rarefied – Dubliners wouldn't stand for it'.

Comfort aside, the real drawcard of the Clarence is Dublin, and the best place to start to get to know this city is the hotel's very own Octagon Bar. At night the Octagon fills up with its eclectic mix of residents and eccentric locals. As Crosbie tells it, 'the brilliant part is that the Clarence has always been part of the Dublin scene and, now that we've redone it, it's still part of Dublin' – which is a polite way of saying that he is really happy they didn't mess it up. This they certainly didn't do. On weekends the bonus of being a hotel guest is that you'll actually get in. Many, many people don't. Hefty guys are stationed on the Liffey, as well as the Temple Bar entrance, to stop the stampede. Even in Ireland, it seems, there's a limit to how many people it takes to make a happy bar.

Then there's the restaurant. The Tea Room, the most talked about restaurant in Dublin, is situated in the impressive space of the hotel's former ballroom. Under the direction of chef Michael Martin (who trained with London's famous Roux brothers) the restaurant serves a surprisingly affordable contemporary cuisine that includes updated, more adventurous versions of Irish classics such as grilled fillet of new season lamb with celeriac purée and black olive jus.

For guests eager to get out of the hotel and explore the city, this is the perfect location. The Clarence is smack in the middle of Temple Bar, a neighbourhood that serves up a heady mix of urban sophistication and grass-roots Irish pub ambience. Return sober from a night out in this area and there's something wrong. But the night life is only half the story. During the day (if you can resist the temptation to stay in nursing a sore head) go out instead and check out one of the best-preserved Georgian cities in the world.

address The Clarence, 6–8 Wellington Quay, Dublin 2, Ireland
telephone (353) 1 670 90 00   **fax** (353) 1 670 78 00
room rates from IR£180 (suites from IR£400)

helvetia & bristol

Helvetia & Bristol is the quintessential Florence hotel. It is timeless and sophisticated, yet in a casual, relaxed manner: a place straight out of E.M. Forster's *A Room With a View*. Located in the very heart of the historic centre of Florence, this 150-year-old establishment was created in the style of an old inner-city palazzo, and has been the discreet favourite of the cognoscenti and aristocracy since before World War I. Famous names such as Igor Stravinsky, Giorgio de Chirico and Gary Cooper, as well as the Danish royal family, have made Helvetia & Bristol their regular home in Florence. And for good reason. The hotel has the style and ambience of a grand but slightly eccentric country house. It personifies everything Florence has to offer: history, beauty, art, people-watching, great food. Sure the hotel also has cable TV with a zillion channels, but wouldn't you really rather be looking at the superb eighteenth-century copy of Raphael's *Madonna della Seggiola* hanging in your room?

The elegant Winter Garden, a perfect spot for afternoon tea, was the favourite meeting place for turn-of-the-century Florentine intellectuals, and until the advent of World War I the hotel's congenial atmosphere and splendid interior drew the wealthy English aristocracy in droves. Originally founded by an old Swiss family, hence the name Helvetia, 'Bristol' was added to make the establishment seem more British. (The aristocracy might have loved Florence, but that didn't mean they were comfortable with the language.)

Today it feels old and timeless, as if it were perfectly preserved. In fact much of what a guest experiences is the result of a fairly recent and concentrated effort to return Helvetia & Bristol to its original ambience and splendour. To do this, architects Fausta Gaetani and Patrizia Ruspoli have, since 1987, steadfastly and painstakingly travelled around the country visiting auctions, markets and antique shops in order to unearth the period pieces which lend the hotel its particular charm. Taking their inspiration from both the Tuscan and English elements of the hotel's heritage they furnished these public and private spaces with carpets, furniture and paintings that evoke a grand late nineteenth-century atmosphere. Incredibly, their efforts are totally undetectable. Everything is as it has always been – or at least feels that way. No wonder French *Vogue Décoration* magazine awarded it the 1990 trophy for the world's finest hotel decor.

From auctions and markets all over Italy, the architects have assembled an array of exquisite antiques

Polished terracotta floors with grey granite inlay express the local character of the Helvetia & Bristol

Intimate and eccentric, the Bristol restaurant serves local Tuscan dishes by chef Francesco Casu

Afternoon tea is a time-honoured tradition in the hotel's famous Winter Garden

Curtains of fine antique Venetian lace adorn the windows of the ground-floor Bristol restaurant

The Winter Garden, meeting place for the Florentine intelligentsia for the past hundred years

Congenial and inviting the atmosphere and decor may well be, but do not forget that this is Florence, city of the Medici – an unrelentingly picturesque place and a city made for exploring, preferably on foot. It is every visitor's cultural responsibility, no less, to see as much as possible. This is a task made all the easier by the Helvetia & Bristol's extraordinary location between Piazza della Repubblica and Via Tornabuoni, only a stroll away from Brunelleschi's Duomo, the River Arno and the Ponte Vecchio, with its many tiny jewelry boutiques. Provided you can tear yourself away from the hotel's stylish interior, there is no better place for embarking on a mission of discovery in this museum-like city. Only when you're tired, and your mind cannot possibly take in any more Renaissance finery, will you have earned that table at Caffè Gilli on Piazza della Repubblica, where you can watch life go by while you enjoy a delicious *panino* and a soothing Campari. Walking around, taking it all in: this is what Florence is all about.

But if Florence is about sightseeing, it is also of course about eating. What, after all, is a visit to anywhere in Italy without taking time to savour the food? The local cuisine is Tuscan, and one of the best places to start is the hotel's very own Bristol Restaurant, a small, elegant space of refined furniture and decorated with crazy 'grotto' chandeliers that used to hang in an eccentric aristocrat's villa on the island of Capri, off Naples. The food is as creative as the decor. Chef Francesco Casu has taken the old recipes of Tuscan tradition and brought them into a modern culinary context. Tuscan specialities include *fettunta* (bread grilled with garlic and oil) as well as a special tomato soup, pasta with beans, breast of pigeon with spinach salad and almond-milk ice cream. All dishes are based on fresh, local and (rare in today's worldwide supermarket mentality) *seasonal* produce. A nod to contemporary health-conscious lifestyles is short cooking time and low fat content. (The alternative would be a gym. In Florence? God forbid!)

address Helvetia & Bristol, Via dei Pescioni 2, 50123 Florence, Italy
telephone (39) 55 287 81 4   **fax** (39) 55 288 35 3
room rates from L490,000 (suites from L890,000)

the peninsula

The 'Pen' is an institution. The history of Hong Kong itself can be traced through the history of this hotel. From the early twenties, when architects were first commissioned to draw up plans for 'the finest hotel east of the Suez', to the present day, when Hong Kong is considered by many to be the New York of the East, only *faster*, the Peninsula has managed to remain *the* place to stay in Hong Kong.

In a city with little time for nostalgia, and where few colonial relics have been preserved, the Peninsula is the big exception – a historic building that is representative of Hong Kong's past as well as its present. This is a hotel that has never let its grand status get in the way of keeping ahead. The Pen was the first to cater to the overland trade in the twenties (when a first-class train trip from London took ten days, running via Calais, Paris, Moscow, Beijing and Shanghai); first to entertain the stars of Hollywood in the thirties (Charlie Chaplin and Paulette Goddard); first to open a disco in the sixties. In the seventies the Pen assembled the world's largest fleet of Rolls-Royces to transport guests from the airport in style, and in the nineties it was first to invite innovative French designer Philippe Starck to design a restaurant and bar for Hong Kong's in-crowd.

Like many of the hotels featured in this book, the Peninsula is a family business. It all started with two brothers of Jewish-Iraqi descent, Elly and Ellis Kadoorie. Ellis settled in Shanghai in 1880, while his elder brother Elly set himself up in business in Hong Kong. Over the next two decades the Kadoorie brothers achieved success in banking, rubber plantations, electric power utilities and real estate, and gained a major share-holding in Hong Kong Hotels Limited. By the time Sir Ellis was knighted in 1917 (he was also a generous patron of charities, another family tradition) Hong Kong Hotels Ltd's prestigious properties included the Peak and the Repulse Bay Hotels in Hong Kong; the Astor House, the Palace Hotel and the Majestic in Shanghai; and the Grand Hotel Wagons Lits in Beijing.

The Peninsula, the jewel in the family crown, was completed in 1928. Twelve years later the baton passed to the next generation when Lawrence (later Lord) Kadoorie, son of Sir Elly, became chairman of the board, to be replaced in 1946 by his brother Horace. With the loss of the Shanghai properties to the government of the People's Republic of China in 1949, the Peninsula became the unchallenged flagship of the company.

The hotel changed with the times, with no less than four modernizations in four decades – some successful, some not (Scandinavian-style interiors introduced in the sixties were universally disliked). But the driving force remained constant: a Kadoorie had to be behind the wheel.

By the time three thousand revellers gathered in 1988 to celebrate the Pen's sixtieth birthday, however, the grand old lady was showing her age. It was up to the latest Kadoorie, the Hon. Michael D. Kadoorie, son of Lord Lawrence, to bring this venerable establishment into the twenty-first century. His response was a daring scheme to add a thirty-storey tower to the original structure. This was to house another 130 rooms, a spectacular swimming pool and spa (designed by Orlando Diaz-Azcuy), a helipad lounge (by Denton Corker Marshall) and a highly innovative new restaurant.

The idea for the two-storey rooftop restaurant was sparked by Kadoorie's visit to Madrid's Teatriz, designed by Philippe Starck. The theatricality and imagination of Teatriz made a powerful impression on Kadoorie. And although Starck had by then announced that he was doing no more restaurants, he was sufficiently intrigued by Kadoorie's novel idea for 'a brasserie for the twenty-first century' in Hong Kong to make an exception. The result, called Felix, has become one of the most photographed restaurants in the world. Starck designed everything, from the chairs to the chinaware. And the loos famously offer the best views of Hong Kong. The food, predictably, is as adventurous as the design – a mix of Pacific ingredients and styles in dishes such as citrus-miso seared wild salmon, and coconut macadamia nut prawn sticks.

But perhaps the *Asian Wall Street Journal* can be credited with the most astute observation on what it is that keeps the Pen ahead of the game: 'it isn't the food that attracts the motley array of patrons,' it commented, 'what attracts the clientele is the clientele'.

address The Peninsula, Salisbury Road, Kowloon, Hong Kong

telephone (852) 2366 6251 **fax** (852) 2722 4170

room rates from HK$2,900 (suites from HK$5,200)

blakes

When actors Jack Nicholson and Robert de Niro or designers Jean-Paul Gaultier and Christian Lacroix stay at Blakes they do so for two reasons: the hotel's policy of offering its clients absolute privacy, and the highly individual style of designer Anouska Hempel … not necessarily in that order.

Ever the perfectionist, Anouska Hempel still supervises every detail of every room, from the silk carpets to the arrangement of flowers. Of the fifty-two guest suites, in colours ranging from crisp clean white to black, mustard, gold, lavender or deep cardinal red, the common design thread is the uninhibited mix of antiques from all ages and from around the world. Like the contents of a caravanserai, there are pieces from Russia, India, Turkey and Eastern Europe scattered throughout the hotel. 'Ultimately, Hempel says, 'I see the role of this place as being able to make dreams a reality'. And converting dreams into reality at Blakes includes a special service for guests whereby faithful reproductions of many of the antiques featured in the rooms are available to purchase. Whether it's a Biedermeier table or a walnut chair or a Rajasthani village meeting table, they are either reproduced by her own team of highly specialized craftsmen or she will use her network of sources to find something very similar – a skill no doubt acquired in her days as an antique dealer. This is a whole new definition of the idea of guest service – designers more often want to conceal their sources than share them – and just one reason why Blakes is so renowned.

Created from two Victorian mansions in South Kensington in the late seventies, Blakes has become one of the most enduring examples of a highly individual hotel to be found anywhere in the world: not just a collection of fanciful, extraordinary bedrooms but a smaller, more intimate version of a grand hotel, complete with an independently successful restaurant and a very popular bar.

The restaurant, called simply Blakes, is as theatrical and imaginative as the rest of the hotel. Decorated in the style of 'an opium den managed by Coco Chanel' (in the memorable words of *Condé Nast Restaurant Guide*), the black walls, distressed leather, bamboo and masses of cushions set the scene for food that includes a perfectly prepared wild mushroom risotto, Blakes blinis with golden beluga, Sichuan duck roasted with salt and pepper, and chicken and crab Fabergé (tied together in the shape of an egg with a strand of seaweed).

The food follows the same 'global gypsy baroque' inspiration as the decor.

Ultimately, the unique experience of Blakes is a result of Anouska Hempel's legendary ability to get things done. 'She's like a general', says Eleanor Lambert, author of New York's Best Dressed list, 'every day she gets up and goes out to conquer'. And she has conquered in many directions. Antique dealer, actress, dress designer, landscape gardener, interior designer and commercial designer, she has spread her imagination like the tentacles of an octopus in as many directions as it can go, including the design of the Louis Vuitton flagship store in the Place Saint-Germain-des-Prés in Paris, the headquarters of BSkyB Television in London, a contemporary makeover of a traditional 85-foot Turkish gulete or boat, and the creation of a range of twenty-seven pens launched by Louis Vuitton in early 1997. As famous photographer Mario Testino will tell you, 'she gets more done in a year than most people achieve in a lifetime'.

Which is just as well considering plans in the works include a Blakes Hotel in Amsterdam (set in a rare 1850s canal-front Empire building with a courtyard garden) and the design of houses scattered all over the globe, from a penthouse in New York to an apartment on the Bosphoros in Istanbul. But it all started with Blakes, a collection of fantasy rooms that run the decorative gamut from Venetian boudoir (Claude Montana's favourite) to all-white Maharaja's pied-à-terre. It helps that she is also the owner. 'Nobody can stop me', she says, 'from acquiring an expensive piece of furniture.' And that is what she will do if it will make the particular scheme for a room a success.

This is the key to the enduring attraction of Blakes: an owner who is not prepared to compromise … or to sit still. This place is anything but static. Colours and design schemes are continually added to or painted over because the rooms, despite their intricacy and fantasy, are in Anouska Hempel's mind never finished. A good dream never is.

---

address Blakes, 33 Roland Gardens, London SW7 3PF, UK

telephone (44) 171 370 6701   **fax** (44) 171 373 0442

room rates from UK£155 (suites from UK£375)

the hempel

Who among us is not fascinated by the Zen notion that to achieve serenity and contentment we must jettison the baggage we schlepp around in daily life? The premise is that we clutter our lives with scores of meaningless possessions. They become a burden and soon we are enslaved to them. Without any possessions – or at least with just the bare minimum – we can once again be free to enjoy ourselves and our lives.

It sounds a reasonable proposition, and could even be true, but only the very, very brave among us would take everything we own to the tip in order to test it out. A more sensible option is to check into the Hempel, for here is a hotel where you can sample 'minimalism'. The Hempel is named after London-based design dynamo Anouska Hempel, a.k.a. Lady Weinberg, who made her name in the world of Hip Hotels with her other London creation, Blakes. To create the Hempel she set up her own team of architects (AH Designs) and worked side by side with them for three exhausting years. The result is a hotel that is cool, white and empty on a monumental scale, a place of Zen-like simplicity. Set into a row of five enormous Edwardian townhouses in the previously forgotten but now up-and-coming area of Bayswater, just north of Hyde Park, it is the embodiment of Lady Weinberg's belief that space is the ultimate luxury in a big city.

Yet, while the Hempel welcomes guests with its acres of white space, it is certainly not a cold or clinical environment. The lobby, described by *Harpers & Queen* as 'larger than an Olympic size swimming pool', is entirely paved in oversize squares of classic Portland limestone and distinguished by a series of geometric cutout spaces that admit pools of warm sunlight. At night, it glows with the light and warmth from two very long, very low and very 'horizontal' hearths that must surely rank as the most elegant fireplaces of any hotel in the world.

The whole interior was conceived according to an oriental concept of simplicity. 'For ten years I've wanted to create this kind of hotel', explains Hempel. 'It's the result of a desire for radical change.' Yet while it is radically different from Blakes, there is still a consistency of approach, for both designs are based on the marriage of occidental and oriental. Eastern influences are reflected in the collection of mahogany umbrella stands from Bombay, artfully arranged along one vast lobby wall.

Tucked into a corner of the Hempel lobby, the library is a space for quiet contemplation

The food at I-Thai mixes Italian, Thai and Japanese cuisine; the presentation is equally exotic

The lobby is a soothingly geometrical, almost temple-like space tiled in acres of limestone

Mahogany umbrella stands from
Bombay and a chair by Australian
designer Marc Newson

The fresh and innovative bathrooms
have been featured extensively in
fashion and interiors magazines

Hidden behind a towering screen
of sand-blasted glass, I-Thai's bar
is a quiet little cocoon of a space

They are also evident in the Indian bullock carts that serve as occasional tables in the uninterrupted symmetry of the sunken lounge, or in the eighty-one potted orchids that define the entrance room. And most obviously, they are apparent in the extraordinary hotel restaurant, I-Thai.

Presided over by a chef formerly of the Oriental Hotel in Bangkok, I-Thai's creative mix of Italian, Thai and Japanese cuisine is served in a fashion perhaps best described as 'edible architectural maquettes' – sculptural presentation so intricately composed that you start your meal with a certain tinge of regret. But I-Thai is not purely a case of cleverly sculptural *théâtre végétal*, the seventeenth-century art of arranging still-lifes to be painted by a master such as Rubens, Van Dyck or Rembrandt. The quality of the food easily matches the standard of the presentation: it's every bit as delicious as it looks.

Even the hotel's garden continues the pared-down theme. Situated in a traditional square opposite the entrance it is almost as if every leaf has been styled to Anouska Hempel's exacting standards. Individual teak and brass recliners – the kind that used to be found on old ocean liners – are positioned between ornamental trees and herb-filled borders. Particularly in summer, the garden adds another dimension to the hotel.

Lady Weinberg has been described as bordering on the fanatical in her attention to detail at the Hempel. That may be true, but as a guest you can only be the beneficiary of her inability to compromise. One room has a floating bed, suspended in the middle of the room like a giant cage; others have a stone bath built into the window recess; in some bathrooms the tap water is illuminated at night by fibre optics. The success of the Hempel emphasizes one gaping truth about minimalism: the more you leave out the better what is left has to be. It is not for the faint-hearted. Less *is* more – more demanding and more exciting.

---

address The Hempel, 31–35 Craven Hill Gardens, London W2 3EA, UK

telephone (44) 171 298 9000 **fax** (44) 171 402 4666

room rates from UK£175 (suites from UK£350)

the metropolitan

The Metropolitan has made Park Lane the coolest place in town, or so claimed at least one recent London newspaper article. Park Lane may be one of the most expensive properties on the English version of Monopoly but unlike, say, Notting Hill it is not these days a cool area with interesting streetlife, shops, restaurants or bars. Yet the Metropolitan – 'a seductive alternative to the nicotine-stained pubs and naff wicker wine bars of the surrounding area' – has certainly made it one of the most popular destinations in town.

But what exactly is it that makes the Metropolitan such a scene? Not first impressions, surely. The Metropolitan is not the kind of place that takes your breath away at first glance … but then neither was it intended to be. According to designer Keith Hobbs, who with partner Linzi Coppick applied a similar formula of refined restraint to the ultra hip Clarence Hotel in Dublin, the aim was to give the Metropolitan a 'buzzy democratic feel'. It was to be a place for locals to meet for a drink and to enjoy dinner as well as a hotel for lifestyle-minded travellers. A cool, calm, airy space is what was envisaged. The design team, United Designers, concentrated on maximizing the light (with big windows), the view (facing Hyde Park) and the space (with rooms larger than your average London hotel room). Plain fabrics, plain blinds and plain walls make a welcome contrast to the usual London formula of reproduction antiques and lots of chintzy curtains. Yet in the case of this hotel, plain + plain + plain does not equal plain. Instead the place exudes an easy sophistication.

A fashion analogy seems inescapable, particularly given the success in the world of retail fashion of the proprietor, Singapore-based Christina Ong. In addition to Donna Karan and Prada concessions, she is the name behind Armani in London. And appropriately, the Metropolitan is rather like an Armani suit. On the rack it may not look much, but it can do amazing things for the person wearing it. The emphasis is on the quality of the materials and on the elegance of the cut. The same is true of the Metropolitan's interiors. The finest materials – special leathers by Bill Amberg, carpets by Helen Yardley, and custom-made furniture such as the dining chairs inspired by Frank Lloyd Wright – combine to create an elegant, understated environment that comes to life with the addition of people. Take the guest rooms: add a suitcase, some clothes and a few travel accessories and the rooms look lived in.

The latest in communication and electronics was given as much thought as the custom-made oak bedheads

An added plus for joggers – Hyde Park is just across the street from the Metropolitan

Co-owned by Robert de Niro, the Metropolitan's Nobu restaurant is a twin to Nobu in TriBeCa, New York

Pale and interesting: rugs by Helen Yardley combine with the odd Chinese antique in the lobby

The Metropolitan is just a short stroll from Bond Street, London's premier shopping address

Furniture is by London-based Bill Amberg, an acclaimed designer in leather

The lobby shop stocks Donna Karan homeware as well as other unexpected treasures

Subtle, subdued colour and clean lines make the rooms completely conducive to modern lifestyles

A small Japanese garden of raked gravel in the window is testament to the attention to detail at the Metropolitan

A sculptural wall clock is one of the few decorative details in an otherwise spare space

In an interior dominated by white, the maple-panelled reception exudes a welcome warmth

Folded leather handles on custom-made oak furniture attest to the commitment to quality

Named after chef Nobuyuki Matsuhisa, Nobu is one of London's most heavily booked restaurants; guests have priority

These custom-designed chairs were inspired by the work of Frank Lloyd Wright

In a city of pubs that close at 11pm, the Met bar has become one of the hottest late-night bars in London

One of the main design criteria was large windows to admit plenty of light

Nobu's repertoire blends Japanese tradition with the ingredients of South American cuisine

The breakfast room, sitting beneath an enormous skylight, doubles as a conference space during the day

In fact, the more you mess it up the *better* it looks. Contrast this with the typically fussy London hotel suite, where the addition of just one bag and a few clothes casually thrown over a chair tips the whole carefully orchestrated still-life into a hopeless clump of clutter. 'In today's world,' explains Keith Hobbs, 'the most valuable commodity is space, and so we wanted to create an air of space … a determined bid for light and simplicity'.

And for once this 'less is more' ethos follows through to the prices: 'we didn't just want financial high flyers drinking Dom Perignon,' says Hobbs. Rooms are not, by London standards, expensive, and in the extremely fashionable restaurant, Nobu, the average price per person is still well within the budget of most London city types. If you can get a table that is. Since its opening in 1997, Nobu has consistently remained one of the most sought-after and high-profile establishments in London. A dinner booking is still almost impossible unless arranged well in advance, though hotel guests do get to jump the queue. (The same goes for the incredibly popular Met bar. People have been known to book a suite just to get into the bar, which in the evening after six o'clock is restricted to members and hotel guests.)

Nobu is the creation of Japanese master chef Nobuyuki Matsuhisa, co-owner with Robert de Niro of the acclaimed Nobu in New York as well as owner of the Matsuhisa restaurant in Los Angeles. Trained as a sushi chef in Tokyo, he travelled throughout South America before eventually establishing a Japanese restaurant in Lima, Peru. He then moved to Alaska, and from there made his way to Los Angeles. Matsuhisa's South American experience accounts for his highly inventive food, which mixes Japanese cuisine with South American spices and ideas. And in the restaurant, as throughout the hotel, the design takes a supporting role, allowing the contemporary London lifestyle to be the real focus of attention.

address The Metropolitan, Old Park Lane, London W1Y 4LB, UK

telephone (44) 171 447 1000 **fax** (44) 171 447 1100

room rates from UK£195 (suites from UK£385)

the portobello hotel

The Portobello doesn't feel like a hotel. It feels more like spending a few days with a rich, funky aunt who happens to live in London's Notting Hill.

For the past two and a half decades the Portobello Hotel has been a true original in a world of overwhelmingly bland hotels. In a way it is the granddaddy of Hip Hotels – the original eccentric outsider that kick-started the current trend for small, offbeat hotels where the interior design is cutting-edge, staff are attentive but discreet, and lobby and rooms alike are intended to feel as intimate as home. This is a nesting experience without the drudgery of tidying up. Established in 1971 by Johnny Ekperegin and designed by Julie Hodges, the Portobello Hotel has consistently been one of the most desirable places to stay in London.

As *Newsweek* magazine recently pointed out, 'the Portobello discovered long ago that the key to success was to play up its quirks and style'. This is a hotel that happily flaunts its own eccentricity. The rooms – unusual, inventive, cosy and very sexy – have that much admired haphazard, casual look that is deemed to be so typically English. This unlikely mishmash of styles attracts an equally unlikely mishmash of legendary guests: like the ageing rocker Alice Cooper, who requested white mice to feed the pet python that he kept in the bath; or Tina Turner, who fell so much in love with the place that she just had to buy the house next door.

Some of the Portobello's rooms have become as legendary as the guests themselves. Take the room with 'the waterworks', for example, a hippy-style suite equipped with what can only be described as a 'Victorian bathing machine': a marvellously eccentric collection of copper pipes, taps and a massive sprinkler, all surgically attached to a turn-of-the-century claw-footed bath. This is a remarkable enough piece in its own right, but picture it standing in the middle of the room on its own little island of black-and-white marble tiles, directly behind a massive round bed tucked into the bay window, and you begin to grasp why this room has become so famous. Then there is the 'four-poster room', which contains an Elizabethan bed so large and high that you need a ladder to climb into it (honest). A canopy painted with clouds reinforces the giddy scale. And for those of us who like to hide in attics there are two fully fledged Moroccan chambers tucked under the roof.

The vivid colours of a Turkish kilim used as a curtain set the sensuous ethnic tone of the Portobello Hotel

Moroccan chandeliers, Victorian antiques, muslin drapes, velvet curtains – this is eclectic, rock-star chic

A round bed set in a bay window overlooking a private park is the focal point of one of the most popular rooms

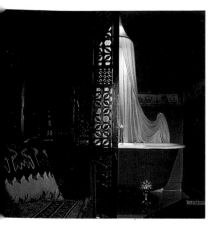

Victorian baths complement the moody oriental atmosphere in the Moroccan-inspired attics

The four-poster room features a gigantic Elizabethan bed complete with oak steps to enable you to climb in

Seashells embedded in a small grotto: the view from the lower-ground-floor restaurant

Moody, dark and dangerously seductive, their rich reds and layers of carpets and cushions evoke the atmosphere of a Berber tent.

Unlike most establishments that cater to the elite, the Portobello Hotel recognizes that 'elite' does not necessarily mean rich. So in a democratic spirit, it also includes rooms that are realistically affordable. Single rooms (ominously referred to as 'cabins', admittedly) do not exactly spoil the guest with space, but the design and decor is no less inventive. Equipped with an extravagantly tented campaign bed, a cabin looks like a place Napoleon might have bedded down for the night. The less romantically inclined might be tempted to dismiss a Portobello cabin as nothing more than a tent bed in a closet; but what do definitions matter when you're staying in the middle of London's hippest neighbourhood?

This is the heart of Notting Hill, home to Europe's biggest annual street carnival. At the Portobello Hotel you are only a few paces away from the hectic hustle of the famed Portobello antiques market and the exceptionally cool shopping scene of Westbourne Grove, with some of London's most innovative and famous boutiques, not to mention bars, cafés and restaurants. This is the area offering precisely the kind of London experience that international magazines are currently so enthusiastic about. Whether it's antiques and vintage clothing you are after, or just groceries and people-watching, Notting Hill is a treasure-trove and a parade. It is also a hot spot for the adventurous gourmand. London's cuisine has changed beyond recognition since the days when a quick curry was the most likely (probably the only) choice after a night out at the local pub. This city, Europe's largest, now leads the world in inventive cuisine, and Notting Hill has more than its share of reputation makers. As in all cities, the place to be changes constantly (if not quite as frequently as New York), so the staff at the Portobello Hotel are the best bet for a local update on the latest and greatest.

---

address The Portobello Hotel, 22 Stanley Gardens, London W11 2NG, UK

telephone (44) 171 727 2777 **fax** (44) 171 792 9641

room rates from UK£100 (suites from UK£185)

chateau marmont

Chateau Marmont is a legend. Think of a name, any famous name, from the world of showbiz – past or present, film, music or television – and there's certain to be a Chateau Marmont anecdote, scandal or connection.

This, after all, is where Paul Newman met his wife Joanne Woodward; where Jean Harlow carried on a scandalous affair with Clark Gable while still on honeymoon with cameraman Harold Rosson; where director Billy Wilder offered to sleep in a bath rather than suffer the indignity of staying elsewhere; where Jim Morrison of the Doors, high as a kite, jumped off the roof of a poolside cabana; where tough guy Robert Mitchum was photographed doing the dishes in an apron; and where John Belushi tragically died of a heroin and cocaine overdose.

Chateau Marmont on Sunset Boulevard has been an enduring feature of the Hollywood scene since the early thirties. Unlike the Garden of Allah, the Trocadero, the Mocambo, Schwab's drugstore and all the other star-studded hangouts that sadly no longer exist on Sunset, Chateau Marmont is still around. Ask a member of the older Hollywood set about the Marmont and their eyes will twinkle as if talking about a naughty but likable uncle who once scandalized (and secretly delighted) the family with his outrageous exploits.

But there is a pitfall to being such a legend – the risk of getting stuck in a time warp. Not so Chateau Marmont. It has changed enough to remain current, but not enough to lose what it once had. This tricky balancing act between preservation and renovation is the notable achievement of New-York-based nightclub, hotel and restaurant impresario André Balazs. On buying the legendary LA property in 1991, Balazs was keenly aware of the prosaic reality that a hotel must update and improve or run the risk of attracting an increasingly diminishing circle of clients. That, in commercial terms, would be a certain death spiral. Yet he also faced pressure from a group of hard-core fans (including the likes of photographer Helmut Newton) to lose nothing of what the hotel had.

Thus, keeping in mind the advice of devoted regulars, the decision was made to upgrade, albeit in a manner that it was hoped would be hardly noticeable. This was no easy task. André Balazs rejected three separate schemes before settling finally on the combined talents of interior designer Fernando Santangelo and production designer Shawn Hausman.

Lamps at Chateau Marmont reflect the theatrical flair of interior designer Fernando Santangelo

The lobby is a popular hang-out for actors summoned to the hotel for a script reading

A fountainhead in the courtyard of a building modelled after the Château Amboise on the Loire

The generous proportions of the rooms reveal the building's original intended use as upmarket Hollywood apartments

Impossible to label, the salon's interior is timelessly appropriate to the lofty dimensions of its beamed space

Bathrooms, wherever possible, are a carefully restored version of the thirties originals

Black-and-white pictures in the 'thirties' phone booths are a reminder of the hotel's legendary history

The funky forties furniture, found by production designer Shawn Hausman, preserves the old Hollywood ambience

Despite being on Sunset Boulevard, Chateau Marmont is blessed with views of green from all sides

The vaguely forties ambience of the newly renovated suites is perfectly appropriate to the hotel's vintage

The restaurant is a ludicrously intimate place that seats no more than twenty and serves French-Californian food

The colonnaded private courtyard is a popular spot for breakfast, a quiet coffee or a late afternoon drink

The salon, in contrast to the guest rooms, is purposefully dark, moody and gothic

Embroidered Frette linen hints at the luxurious attention to detail: there is more to this hotel than reputation

The gym, a recent addition, is hidden away in the spacious, air-conditioned attic

In contrast to the dark and moody lobby the rooms are bright and white, furnished in a *faux* forties style

Gothic shapes and a time-worn patina mix well with most guests' preference for basic designer black

Gothic, gothic, gothic – despite Chateau Marmont's laid-back image, the attention to detail is anything but

Their contribution, exactly as Balazs requested, was to make the Marmont look as you would imagine it has always looked. Design was used to create an illusion (appropriately enough for a Hollywood hotel): the illusion that it has always been so. And it has worked … without skipping a beat. Regulars still wouldn't dream of staying anywhere else (enjoying, no doubt, the added extras of room service, not an option in the old Marmont, and an efficient telephone system, unlike the infamous 'pot luck' exchange of the past). And new clientele are attracted by the forties-style glamour of the rooms and the undimmed reputation.

The fact that Chateau Marmont was never intended to be a hotel is probably what makes it such an attractive one. Built in the twenties as an earthquake-proof imitation of the royal Château Amboise on the Loire in France (its foundations are on solid rock), the layout and size of the rooms at the Marmont owe their generous proportions to the simple fact that they were originally designed as apartments.

Perhaps this also explains why some guests check in for months at a time. Robert de Niro lived in the penthouse for two years, and Keanu Reeves doesn't even own a place in LA, preferring instead the comfort of the Marmont. The most famous recent name to make the Chateau Marmont a long-term West Coast habit was writer Dominick Dunne, who stayed there for the entire duration of the O.J. Simpson trial, which he covered for *Vanity Fair*.

In the best Hollywood tradition, Chateau Marmont is the kind of place where you can avoid leaving your room for weeks on end and no one will think anything of it. Room service, as might therefore be expected, does a roaring trade in this hotel. In fact so few guests venture out that the lobby, terrace and dining room are hardly ever too crowded – a very pleasant bonus for the odd guest *not* interested in locking him or herself away. Whatever it is that Chateau Marmont has going for it, one thing is certain: this is one Hollywood legend that doesn't disappoint in real life.

address Chateau Marmont, 8221 Sunset Boulevard, Hollywood, CAL 90046, USA

telephone (1) 213 656 10 10 or (1) 800 CHATEAU **fax** (1) 213 655 53 11

room rates from US$210 (suites from US$415)

mondrian

The Mondrian is very LA – it's big, it's glamorous, it's pretentious and it's filled with stars. This latest addition to the Ian Schrager stable of Hip Hotels, the fourth hotel collaboration between Schrager and his star designer Philippe Starck, has truly captured the 'top down, sunglasses on' spirit of Los Angeles.

Located up on Sunset (where else?), looking across all of LA, the Mondrian is almost a cliché of the quintessential LA experience. First there is the pool: not very large, it is true, more for dipping than swimming, but thanks to the extensive deck surrounding it and the quirky manner it has been furnished, an extremely popular place to hang out. It feels more like an outdoor lobby. The whole poolside experience is *Melrose Place* with more space, better design, and more inspiring dialogue. All you need are sunglasses, a sarong and your room key (how else can you show that yes, you are actually staying here, not just hanging out by the pool like so many of the other beautiful people?). The waitresses look good in their sarongs, and so do the chairs – for even the furniture follows the laid-back dress code. Who else but Philippe Starck would consider wicker wing chairs draped with brightly coloured sarongs as poolside furniture?

By and large the attitude at the Mondrian is 'see and be seen'. But if you're not in the mood to be ogled while having lunch, Coco Pazzo, the Mondrian's restaurant, provides privacy in a very Starck fashion by hiding tables behind a disciplined row of eight-foot-high flower pots – Godzilla-size versions of your typical kitsch terracotta pots planted with bay trees that provide welcome shade. At night, if the urge to be seen strikes again, the Mondrian has the hottest bar in town, the Sky Bar. Built in a style best described as a cross between an Adirondack rowing shack and a Bali beach club, this quirky outdoor pavilion is the place to be. If you can get in, that is. If you're a local and you ain't a star – good luck! One of the distinct benefits of being a guest is that you get to hang out and do some serious mingling in a place that normally wouldn't admit you. Just make sure you keep hold of that room key.

Bizarre but entertaining, the scene at the Mondrian is thoroughly LA. Any time it gets too much, the rooms are the perfect retreat. Vast, immaculate, all-white spaces (bar a touch of green and a light-grey carpet) they have that 'poolside cabana' feel – more like a Malibu apartment than a hotel room. *Wallpaper* recently voted them the best in the world.

115

The Mondrian has instigated a trend whereby many pieces in the rooms are for sale, including the potted orchid

In the lobby bar, bowls of fresh fruit are topped up all day to encourage a healthy LA way of life

The terracotta pot is a recurrent design theme and a welcome change from inane beach umbrellas

Rooms are bright and big, with a full kitchen and breakfast space as well as a living area

This, believe it or not, is the concierge's desk. If you have travel needs or plans just sit at the table

Although the pool is not particularly large, it offers spectacular views over Los Angeles

The polished, modern environment of the lobby includes eccentric design anomalies, such as a huge log

Coco Pazzo, Mondrian's restaurant, is the West Coast twin of the New York restaurant of the same name

White is only right when, as here, the crisp bedlinen is perfectly ironed and immaculately clean

A deep-buttoned conversation corner tucked away in the lobby is vintage Starck

The lobby bar is locked away inside a mobile unit that opens at night to dispense cocktails

The Sky Bar, a separate outdoor pavilion overlooking the pool, is one of the hottest bars in LA

Adjacent to the pool deck, the gym has a free weights room, steam rooms and an assortment of running tracks

Starck's enormous terracotta pots on the outdoor deck are funny and practical, providing shade and privacy

Sari-covered wing chairs, Chinese ceramic stools, and old Bakelite phones are Mondrian's take on lobby furniture

Wicker wing chairs draped in brightly coloured sarongs: Mondrian's alternative to plastic banana chairs

The Mondrian's light-filled lobby bar is a popular place for a casual but stylish breakfast

The pool deck functions like a hotel bar – it's the place where people meet and hang out

Not only are they furnished with a kitchen and charming breakfast nook, but someone has already done the shopping. Stocked with enough provisions for a week, the mini-bar has been expanded into a mini-deli. In fact, the Mondrian takes the whole idea of the hotel doing the shopping for you to a new dimension. We've all seen the polite notices that invite us, if we really like the bathrobe, to *buy* one. The Mondrian invites you, if you really like the hotel, to buy the entire contents of your room. They provide a comprehensive catalogue, as detailed as a home insurance inventory, to help. Everything from the corkscrew to the potted orchid – chairs, plates, cushions, pencil cups, you name it – is listed and priced. Invited to a birthday lunch outside the hotel, I admit that the pretty orchid in a classic terracotta pot had the makings of a terrific present, and who would ever know that it was the result of the hotel's thoughtfulness rather than my own?

There's no question that the Mondrian is a hotel for sybarites. With its indoor–outdoor design chic expressed in a pale palette of white, biscuit and ecru, the Mondrian has a sensual quality that manages to merge the demands of the business traveller with the seduction of a resort. And just as well, because LA is one of those cities, along with Miami, Barcelona and Sydney, where the weather is a vital part of the experience guests demand of the hotel. Nobody would care if a hotel in London lacked a pool, but in LA it's important. And it's these 'I'm here so spoil me' luxury touches that the Schrager-Starck team do so well.

Following a trend that Schrager himself started at the Royalton and the Paramount, the restaurant (Coco Pazzo), the bar (the Sky Bar), even the magazine and newspaper concession are all licensed to independent operators. This inventive bit of delegation ensures the hotel remains a fixture for a steady stream of local customers (who come for the food and ambience) as well as out-of-towners. Ultimately it's what makes the hotel, as Schrager would describe it, 'the nightclub of the nineties'.

address Mondrian, 8440 Sunset Boulevard, West Hollywood CA 90059 , USA

telephone (1) 213 650 89 99   **fax** (1) 213 650 52 15

room rates from US$250 (suites from US$400)

the adelphi

Pedestrians strolling through Flinders lane, the heart of Melbourne's inner city, are liable to experience one of the most peculiar images imaginable if their gaze happens to travel skywards: the glimpse of swimmers doing laps eight storeys above the street. Perhaps stranger still is the view for the swimmers, gazing down at the roofs of taxis and trucks as they're about to make their tumble turns.

Needless to say, the Adelphi's one-of-a-kind cantilevered swimming pool has attracted its fair share of attention since the hotel first opened in 1992. But it would be an injustice to the hotel to dismiss this as nothing more than an attention-grabbing gimmick. In fact, the suspended glass-bottomed lap pool is an appropriate metaphor for the entire hotel: adventurous and unconventional. There is absolutely no aspect of the Adelphi – furnishing, detailing, design or otherwise – that shows any sign of compromise. This is a progressively minded, 'street smart' hotel that says, in design terms, 'if you don't like it, go somewhere else'.

A place as aggressively hip as this may come as a surprise to those unacquainted with Melbourne. This is a city of great cafés, good restaurants, trendy bars and architect-designed night clubs, and design plays a big role in these venues. Melbourne's art and architecture community is thriving, and it shows.

It helps, of course, in the case of the Adelphi, that the architects also happen to be the proprietors. Denton Corker Marshall, the Melbourne-based architectural partnership of John Denton, Bill Corker and Barrie Marshall, is one of the big architecture success stories in the East. With offices in Sydney, Jakarta, Hong Kong, London, Warsaw, Ho Chi Minh City and Tokyo, DCM are responsible for some of the biggest and most innovative architectural projects in Asia, including award-winning Australian embassies in Tokyo and Beijing. Yet despite their size, they are not corporate boys. They remain streetwise, with a passion for design that is reflected in this small project where they have truly put their money where their mouth is.

Playing the dual role of architect and client has allowed DCM not just to invent the space but also to determine the way it is furnished, and they went to considerable effort to translate their distinctive architectural signature into an interior design scheme. The guest rooms are elegant and spare with a black slab bed hovering over a black carpeted floor.

The deceptive achievement of DCM's design is to make the complex look remarkably simple

Only asymmetrical furniture designed by the architects themselves is permitted to interrupt the Zen simplicity of the space

'What's all the fuss?' asks architect Barrie Marshall, 'the pool only sticks out 1½ metres' (even if it is eight storeys up)

Only in a hotel owned, designed and operated by architects would you find pepper and salt mills by Ettore Sottsass

The bathrooms are as minimal as it gets, with polished Chinese granite floors and stainless-steel sinks

White bed linen, white Roman blinds: there is something inescapably sexy about such smooth simplicity

A view across the lap pool towards the Adelphi Roof Club, a members-only bar popular late at night

The restaurant interior is interrupted only by suspended photographs of architecture by John Gollings

The restaurant is all about polished concrete, intersecting angles and lots of white: an architect's space

The Adelphi's bedheads are simplicity itself, just sheets of ash-faced plywood, next to stainless-steel side tables

Intersecting planes of bright colour define the exterior and the glass-bottomed pool

Poolside on the roof is one of several places to hang out at the Adelphi, especially for sun-worshippers

The Adelphi café in the hotel's basement, where breakfast starts with the best caffe latte in town

The Adelphi is situated in Flinders Lane, home to Melbourne's top art dealers

The building's gutsy origin as an inner-city warehouse suited the architects' no-frills plans perfectly

An urban warehouse conversion is not what most people would expect of Melbourne

Even the restaurant chairs came off the drawing boards of Denton Corker Marshall, the architects and proprietors

A sandblasted glass partition wall with stainless-steel studs to hang a bathrobe from

Bedside tables are simple wedges of satin-polished stainless steel suspended from the wall, and the all-white walls are uninterrupted save by a single, abstract, angular piece of furniture in multicoloured leather. The bathrooms have even more of an edge. Floors of black Chinese granite paired with a long, sleek, stainless-steel slab, indented in the middle to form a sink-like trough, are pure simplicity, a Zen space to shower and shave.

Throughout the hotel there is not a single item, doorknobs included, that didn't come off the drawing boards of DCM. And the all-white café-restaurant downstairs and the black bar on the roof are like nothing you have seen before. The bar, only open at night, has the hotel's best view over Melbourne's metropolis, and the all-black interior – black rubber floor, black leather furniture and black-painted walls – only accentuates the view. In the basement, or rather the *souterrain* (for it still has windows to the street), the all-white interior of the café-restaurant, with its unique, custom-made

chairs of white nylon, is softened by the light grey of a bleached concrete floor, with the DCM trademark of brightly coloured metal bars dissecting the space.

The food, perhaps unexpectedly, is just as good as the design. The café-restaurant of the Adelphi is one of very few places in Melbourne to have been awarded three 'chefs hats' by *The Age*, the city's most respected newspaper (the equivalent to a Michelin star in Europe). This distinction has ensured that the place is full from eight in the morning until midnight.

On top of this, the Adelphi enjoys the best location in the city. Situated on the most avant-garde street in Melbourne (the address of all the major art galleries), it is around the corner from the major theatres and night clubs, and next door to the city's best shopping street, Bourke Street. The odd guest has been known to bang a shin against the stainless steel bedside table, but that's the only downside to all this uncompromising design. And surely it's better to be a little black and blue than to be bored.

---

address The Adelphi, 187 Flinders Lane, Melbourne, Victoria 3000, Australia

telephone (61) 3 9650 75 55   fax (61) 3 9650 27 10

room rates from A$200 (suites from A$350)

the prince of wales

Of all the cities on the Pacific Rim, Melbourne may be the most enigmatic. Beyond being the site of the '56 Olympics and the Australian Open tennis tournament, what do we know about this city? Very little, probably; but that lack of preconceived ideas is what makes it interesting. Not as visually idyllic as Sydney, with its splendid harbourside location, Australia's second city has always had to compensate for lack of good looks with personality. Sydney may be more beautiful, but Melbourne is more fun.

It is also the second largest Greek city in the world. Only Athens is bigger. With over a million people of Greek descent, the culture of the southern Mediterranean is well and truly in the blood. Maybe that's why eating and drinking are such serious pastimes. The quality of wine, vegetables and fruit is a vocabulary with which most residents are conversant. And in a city of sophisticated choices in eating and drinking, design is an essential ingredient. If it tastes good it has to look good and vice versa. Presentation is taken as seriously as the food. And no one has been more successful with this formula than restaurant entrepreneur John van Haandel. A decade ago he took a rundown hamburger and fries concession on the beach

and transformed it into the Stokehouse, one of the most successful restaurants in the country, and one that cleverly caters to all of Melbourne's food-loving public, not just the elite. Upstairs is a restaurant with a Gauguin-inspired design that consistently showcases the best chefs in the southern hemisphere, while the downstairs brasserie provides simple Mediterranean fare with a beachside location at a budget price.

But van Haandel's Stokehouse isn't alone in realizing the potential of the formerly derelict and dangerous seaside location of St Kilda. Like Miami's South Beach, it used to be the home of drunks, drug addicts and the odd intrepid artist or architect drawn to the area by its irresistible collection of Victorian beachside architecture. Slowly, over the past fifteen years, place after place has been transformed into smart bars, trendy clubs and chic restaurants, making St Kilda one of the most exciting areas of the city. It was only a matter of time before a hotel entered the equation, and van Handel is well and truly first in, best dressed.

Located in a former workers' pub on Fitzroy Street, the main drag leading to the beach (the Melbourne equivalent of Miami's Ocean Drive), the Prince of Wales is the classic

Aussie pub on the outside and anything but the classic Aussie pub on the inside. The interior reflects the new Australian mentality – a sophisticated Mediterranean-style approach with a shot of Asian influence. Organic 'sixties' furniture by Australian designer Grant Featherstone is combined with Thai silk, lamps inspired by Noguchi and minimal furniture by young local designers. The architect responsible, Alan Powell, was one of the first to move into the area at a time when it was still derelict, so his street credentials are impeccable. He has completed several commercial projects in the area (all of them restaurants and bars) and so has had plenty of opportunity to refine his approach to a neighbourhood that is rapidly becoming Melbourne's hippest.

A stone's throw from the beach (Melbourne, alas, is on a bay, so no surf) and not much further from Albert Park, the setting of the Australian Grand Prix, this is the place that many locals head to on weekends for coffee, lunch or just to meet for a drink. And the new kid in town, with the hottest bar and the most talked about restaurant, is the Prince of Wales. Mink, its innovative bar, specializes in vodka, serving forty-three different brands of it, which are as much part of the interior design as the furniture. Currently hogging the Australian press inches devoted to the hottest and hippest, Mink is not just the place be, but probably one of the most original bars in the urban context. It is light years away from the slosh and swill as much as you can, as fast as you can, six-o'clock-closing culture of Australian pubs in the fifties and sixties. While the bar is appropriately Russian baroque red, the restaurant, like the rooms, is more pared down, with just the odd swag of oriental colour and a fine repertoire of contemporary, Australian-designed furniture. Along with Barcelona, Miami and Sydney, Melbourne now ranks among the few capitals that can offer the best of both urban and beach living.

address The Prince of Wales Hotel, 2B Acland Street, St Kilda, Melbourne, Australia
telephone (61) 3 9536 1111 **fax** (61) 3 9536 1183
room rates from A$185

hotel astor

Blame it on age, vanity, the ozone layer, or all three, but an increasing number of people coming to Miami aren't interested in a beach holiday. They may sit by the pool with a book, but baking in the sun on the beach is not part of their agenda. There is too much else to do.

Ever since the early eighties, when a handful of creative types rediscovered the dilapidated Art Deco legacy of Ocean Drive in what was then one of Miami's most run-down and dangerous areas, Miami's South Beach has seen a renaissance of a magnitude unparalleled in any other US city. Pushed along by the television series *Miami Vice*, a new international airport, and the monumental city architecture of Miami-based design group Architectonica, a former wasteland has, within the space of a decade, been turned into one of the most interesting cities in America. Lured by the weather and the distinctly Latin atmosphere, the in-crowds from New York and other northern cities now regularly make their way down to Miami.

One of the most tangible benefits of this hip renaissance is the food. South Beach offers an almost bewildering choice of places to eat and drink. As in most big cities, the pecking order changes quite frequently. But one thing almost everyone agrees on, including the *New York Times*, *Vogue* and *Forbes*, is that one of the finest restaurants in South Beach, if not the best, is Astor Place. Set in a magnificent Art-Deco-inspired atrium space designed by acclaimed restaurant architect Morris Nathanson, the restaurant features the culinary talents of executive chef Johnny Vinczencz. The food, variously described as 'New Floridian' or 'Caribbean cowboy', is certainly inventive, though thankfully not to the point that it becomes confusing. My favourite? The wild mushroom pancakes: buttermilk hotcakes layered with portobello mushrooms and served with a balsamic 'syrup' and sundried-tomato butter.

New York Times critic Mitchell Owens is convinced that the food is the reason people stay here, and he is probably right. But there's more to the Astor than great food. Ever since Karim Masri – a Lebanese-born, Paris-educated ex-investment banker – bought the squalid, run-down hulk of a streamlined 1936 Art Deco hotel, he has cut no corners in creating a sleek, elegant environment that emulates the understated style of the world's best concierge hotels. The result is a place that, in the words of design team Patrick Kennedy and Peter Page, 'is all about comfort, intelligence and romance – not about being a design statement'. Described by US *Vogue* as 'delightfully low profile', the cool style of the Astor reflects not only 'an eye for expensive detail' but also a desire to create a place that will be impervious to the fickle finger of fashion. With slip-covered chairs in Belgian linen, a sand-beige colour scheme and timber joinery by leading French marine cabinet makers Chantiers Baudet (who also fitted out Barneys in New York) the interiors of the forty guest rooms are a seductive cross between a luxury yacht and an Armani boutique. It is almost impossible to imagine that just ten years ago this place was a crack house.

The Astor has not been alone in cleaning up its act. The surrounding neighbourhood has also been considerably rejuvenated. Located diagonally across the street from the hotel is the recently opened Wolfsonian Foundation Museum. Converted from an exotic 1926 furniture warehouse inspired (believe it or not)

by the sixteenth-century library of Salamanca, the Wolfsonian showcases one of the world's most extensive collections of decorative, architectural, graphic and propaganda art of the late nineteenth and early twentieth centuries. The museum had such a major hit with its inaugural exhibition 'The Arts of Reform and Persuasion 1885–1945', a poignant look at the power of design to sell messages, that it is now in the enviable position of being a cultural exporter, with the award-winning exhibition on extended international tour. And the other museums in South Beach have no intention of being left behind. The Bass Museum of Art, for example, has announced plans to expand its Art Deco palazzo just off Lincoln Road with an eight-million-dollar addition designed by Arata Isozaki that will double the museum's space.

All this is in a city where officials, just two decades ago, thought the best way for a comeback was to demolish the old Deco buildings and replace them with high-rise casino hotels.

---

address Hotel Astor, 956 Washington Avenue, Miami Beach, FL 33139, USA
telephone (1) 305 531 80 81 or (1) 800 270 49 81   **fax** (1) 305 531 31 93
room rates from US$145 (suites from US$320)

marlin

The newly revamped Marlin mixes a funky futuristic style with splashes of Caribbean colour in a design that seems curiously reminiscent of the 1962 James Bond film *Doctor No*. And oddly enough, there is a connection. Ian Fleming, creator of James Bond, was the owner of a Jamaican estate called 'Goldeneye'. This estate was recently purchased by the founder of Island Records Chris Blackwell, who also happens to be the highly successful proprietor of a string of South Beach Hip Hotels, among them the Marlin.

In the film, Doctor No is the crazed scientist and master criminal who has built himself a mysterious island retreat in the Caribbean from where he intends to hold the world to ransom by threatening to unleash weapons of mass destruction. (No points for guessing who stops him.) But Doctor No is not just mad and evil; he is also extremely stylish. *Wallpaper* magazine would kill for a pad like his: a sexy combination of futuristic laboratory with acres of stainless steel, banks of computer screens (pretty advanced for 1962), thousands of flashing buttons, pared-down monochromatic furniture, streamlined grotto walls, and girls in silk kimonos continually disappearing behind big sliding doors.

The new Marlin Hotel could almost be Doctor No's Miami pied-à-terre. The shiny stainless steel has reappeared in the futuristic styling of the lobby; the computer screens have metamorphosed into giant television sets permanently tuned to MTV; and the guest rooms, with their built-in furniture, rounded walls and monochromatic colour scheme, resemble the organic grotto spaces of Doctor No's island hideaway. Alas, there are no smooth-sliding automatic doors, but Marlin guests *are* handed an armload of remote controls to operate the video, the stereo and the cutting-edge-technology web TV, which gives them internet access as well as an e-mail address.

The designer responsible for realizing this fantasy is herself a character straight out of a James Bond film. Permanently dressed in black, with silver hair and big black glasses, Barbara Hulanicki knows a thing or two about creating environments that attract a lot of attention. She was the name behind Biba, London's legendary but now defunct department store where the likes of David Bowie, Elton John and other glam rock stars once bought their silver platform shoes and pink Lurex T-shirts.

But it's not just design that makes the Marlin hip. A genuine effort has been made to define a new hotel experience. What good is it, for instance, to have a stereo in every room if there is nothing to play? Not a problem if the proprietor used to own a record label. A funky selection of brand new CDs sits next to each stereo (all available to buy should should you become too hooked) and each room throbs to a different beat. The noise? No problem. The rooms, as you would expect from a designer used to catering for rock stars, are amply soundproofed.

In fact the Marlin is very much a music hotel. There are fully equipped recording studios located at the far end of the lobby, and the hotel manager, Ian Innocent, doesn't arrive until later in the day because he also happens to be one of the hottest DJs in Miami. During the day you can listen to him on a South Beach radio station; in the evening he's behind the reception desk or in the Marlin Bar, where he will usually spin some discs as the scene, in

a regular nightly ritual, starts to hot up. And the scene at the Marlin goes on till the early hours of the morning. There's even a special reclining pit adjacent to the bar called the Shabeen lounge: a cave-like space, piled high with oversized cushions covered in colourful Caribbean fabrics. The ambience at the Marlin, as distinct from the frenetic salsa tempo of most of Ocean Drive, is best described as 'Cubarean': a spicy mix of hot Latin and cool Caribbean that defines the food as well as the music.

During the day the Marlin has the kind of unhurried, lazy attitude normally associated with the Caribbean islands. Just sitting in the lobby with a cappuccino can be entertainment enough. Johnny Casablanca's modelling agency Elite (the one that fired Naomi Campbell) is on the first floor, so all day long picturesque persons, mostly on rollerblades, glide across the Marlin's original 1930s terrazzo floor on their way to yet another casting for a 'fun in the sun' photo shoot. No wonder Miami attracts the rich, the famous and the curious.

---

address Marlin, 1200 Collins Avenue, Miami Beach, FL 33139, USA

telephone (1) 305 604 50 00 or (1) 800 688 76 78 **fax** (1) 305 673 96 09

room rates from US$195 (suites from US$425)

pelican

Miami is currently the fastest growing city in the US, South Beach is the fastest growing part of Miami, Ocean Drive is the fastest growing street in South Beach, and the Pelican is quite simply the 'fastest' hotel in town.

Nestled in among all the other candy-coloured, streamlined Art Deco hotels of Miami's Ocean Drive, the city's liveliest seaside strip, the Pelican is known as the kooky outsider. Owned and operated by Diesel, the Italian label that has made a mark with its satire on the pretences of the fashion world, this 1950s building in American 'motel' style has become the first expression in interior design of Diesel's unique and very hip sensibility: irreverent, slightly crazed, and fun.

If you really want to be in the thick of things it's impossible to be closer to the action. Next door is Lario's, Gloria Estefan's celebrated Cuban restaurant, two doors down is the News Café, *the* place to have breakfast, upstairs at the Pelican is the Miami chapter of the Ford modelling agency, and just across the street is the most popular stretch of the beach itself – the part with the volleyball nets, the rollerblading track, the never-ending parade of perfect bodies and a cameo role in every other American breakfast-cereal commercial.

Staying at the Pelican is like dressing up. You can be whoever you want to be in a room that dresses up with you. Feeling patriotic? The 'Born in the Stars and Stripes' room is for you. All hot from the music? Book the all-red 'Best Whorehouse' room. Feeling primitive? Try 'Me Tarzan, You Vain'. Spiritual? Spend the night in the 'Jesus Christ Megastar' room. Disco fever? The 'Psychedelicate Girl' room is definitely for you. And there are more – many more. Try 'Love, Peace and Leafforest', 'A Fortune in Aluminum', 'Some Like it Wet', 'Power Flower', 'Decocktail', 'Bang a Boomerang', 'Half-Way to Hollywood', 'Viva Las Vegas' or 'Big Bamboo'. Each and every one of Pelican's rooms is dedicated and designed to a theme. In design language this hotel is saying to you, the guest: 'This is a Latin city. Relax, enjoy yourself and give in to your imagination.'

Thankfully however, fantasy is not delivered at the expense of comfort. There is maid service twice a day, and every room is equipped with TV, video, quality stereo, fridge, and a minimum of two phones (one in the bathroom). Special examples of attention to detail include industrial ceiling fans and recycled oak floors (carpet in tropical Miami? No thank you.)

The 'Me Tarzan, You Vain' room
– a wild bit of Africa Graphica
on Ocean Drive

Bottle-cap baroque: the mirror is perfect
for the 'Executive Sixties' suite of
Miami's Pelican Hotel

Extravagant it may be, but the bathroom
of the madcap penthouse suite is believe
it or not its most sedate space

The 'Executive Sixties' suite with
a view of the beach is all colour
and fantastic plastic

'Best Whorehouse' – definitely
a blinds-down, lights-out
kind of a room

Designer Magnus Ehrland collected
what must be the world's greatest
hoard of garage-sale kitsch

The Pelican doesn't have a traditional
lobby – instead, very sensibly, there
is a bar in the hotel entrance

'Born in the Stars and Stripes' is perfect
for patriotic Republicans (not that
you're likely to meet one here)

Bring your sunglasses: 'Psychedelicate
Girl' is a room for those with a taste for
the wild visuals of the Pop Art sixties

The 'Executive Forties' suite – a long slender room with a corner view of the beach and Ocean Drive

Each room at the Pelican has its own theme and colour scheme: tropical green in the 'Executive Forties' suite

A driftwood lamp is exactly the right kind of kitsch to dress up the 'Executive Fifties' suite

Ruby red and completely over the top, the 'Best Whorehouse' is one of Pelican's most popular rooms

A colourful mosaic typical of the late fifties/early sixties decorates the window sill of the 'Executive Sixties' suite

A twenties poster for a now-defunct brand of cigarettes (in case you wondered where they got the name)

'Up, Up and Away' – a room entirely decorated with bits and pieces of aeroplane

The restaurant's unique style is part roadside diner, part gambling shack, and part industrial warehouse

The 'Executive Fifties' suite: a *Blue Hawaii* kind of interior that faces the beach and Ocean Drive

Life as a guest is certainly an original experience. The fun begins when the sweaty cab that dumped you at the curb (Miami taxis are not air-conditioned) leaves you dragging your suitcases through the Pelican's crowded restaurant, swearing under your breath: 'What do you mean there's no lobby?'

This doesn't seem funny at the time but a few days later when you see another pasty newcomer undergo the same initiation, it suddenly feels like an in-joke. According to the hotel, dragging your bags through the restaurant helps break down 'traditional expectations' – and besides, they really *don't* have much of a lobby. They used the space for the restaurant and bar. It's space well used: the casual atmosphere, courtesy of the 'Honolulu, *c.* 1954, enlisted men's drinking club' decor, and the generous portions of simple healthy food make it a very easy place to hang out.

In a crazy but charming way, the Pelican takes a gentle swipe at the kitsch underbelly of Miami. Its design is a cheeky take on the crass commercialism of America and Americana. Swedish designer Magnus Ehrland travelled the globe to assemble what must be the single largest collection of modern retro kitsch in the world and used it to create twenty-five themed rooms that play to every fantasy imaginable.

But the seemingly hodgepodge assembly of garage sale items ranging from hula girl lamps to bright orange gothic dining chairs is more sophisticated than it might seem. To hover on the absolute edge of bad taste, without simply being silly and ugly, is not so easy. Like wearing second-hand clothing, you need a lot of confidence and an innate sense of style to carry it off. To stick your creative neck out in this fashion is daring, and Pelican's stylistic bravery has been rewarded with resounding success. Sure, each room is a spoof on the American dream, but they are also unusual, interesting and above all, lots of fun. This, after all, is a hotel, not a home. Why not enjoy a bit of kookiness while you are away? The Pelican is outrageous, but then so is Miami.

---

address Pelican, 826 Ocean Drive, Miami Beach, FL 33139, USA

telephone (1) 305 673 33 73 **fax** (1) 305 673 32 55

room rates from US$160 (suites from US$280)

the tides

If the Pelican is South Beach's kooky outsider then the Tides is the smooth newcomer. The ten-storey, all-white Tides is the largest and most imposing structure on Ocean Drive, standing in stately contrast to the other rather squat Art Deco hotels lining Miami's most famous beachside strip. Billed as the first *mature* hotel on South Beach, this whitewashed, ocean-side Art Deco classic (originally opened in 1936) is the jewel in Chris Blackwell's imposing collection of South Beach hotels. It was among the first hotels that he acquired a decade ago, but interestingly he opted to develop the smaller properties first, saving this – the best – until last.

To launch into what is widely recognized as the second, more refined stage of the continuing rehabilitation of South Beach, Blackwell decided to draw on the services of John Pringle, something of an expert on hotels that pull a good crowd. Between 1951 and 1961 Pringle owned and operated Round Hill, a Jamaican retreat frequented by the likes of the Kennedys, Richard Avedon, Bing Crosby, Alfred Hitchcock, in fact by just about every luminary of the day. 'The secret,' Pringle will confide, 'is to combine low-key guests with anything but low-key service.' The guests are

encouraged to be laid back … the staff is not. It might sound simple enough, but Pringle himself will readily concede that this is not an easy combination to realize.

A distant cousin of Blackwell, Pringle had previously worked as a consultant for his growing hotel empire, but the Tides is the first project in which his involvement, at Blackwell's insistence, was totally hands-on. Not a cushion, curtain or ashtray has escaped Pringle's microscopic attention to detail. Comfort, in his eyes, is only achieved by getting all the details right, small as well as big. And elegant comfort, the kind that appears effortless, was always his aim. This is design by vigilance – a rigorous and disciplined quest to create the kind of place that will attract people accustomed to a certain quality of life. It is not about dazzling them with glitz and glamour but about conjuring up an atmosphere of effortless sophistication.

The Tides is a confident adult alternative for the traveller who appreciates calm as well as frenzy. Calm is the operative word for this place. In contrast to the hectic salsa-driven pace of Ocean Drive, the lobby is as quiet as a soundproof studio. And it is quiet to the eyes as well as the ears: the place is the architectural equivalent of a summer suit,

all cream, beige and off-white, in natural fibres, set against the pale, polished beauty of the original terrazzo floor.

The quiet elegance of the lobby is an appropriate entrée to the Tides' real drawcard, the rooms – or rather the suites, for they are too big to be called rooms. Large, open, all-white and facing the ocean, each is like a tropical loft, a generous whitewashed space with romantic shutters and a clever design that separates off practical facilities such as the closet, mini-bar and changing room, and so allows the main space to remain beautifully unencumbered. Undoubtedly the most remarkable feature is that they all face the beach. When I first heard this I took it to mean some of the rooms, perhaps even most of them. How could each and every one overlook the beach? The answer lies in a drastic remodelling of the interior architecture. The corridor allowing access to the four rooms on each floor was relocated to run along the back of the building (making it the only hotel space with views of the car park to the rear). This no-compromise approach entailed a radical restructuring and the creation of just 45 rooms from 112, a courageous step that would normally be considered bad mathematics in the hotel trade. But for the guest it makes all the difference in the world. In a warm climate, after all, space is directly related to coolness. And a view of the ocean is what everyone wants.

Keeping cool was also a priority in the design of the fitness centre. In the upper reaches of the building, high enough to pick up any trace of a sea breeze, a corner was simply covered over with an awning. Guests work out there with the weather. El Niño aside, this is a far more attractive proposition than being locked away in the small, sealed, air-conditioned environment of many hotel gyms.

The guiding aim was to create a discreet and tasteful backdrop to the customers, who Pringle believes 'are more important than any design scheme'. 'A hotel is like a play', he will tell you: 'if the cast is good, the play is good'.

---

address The Tides, 1220 Ocean Drive, Miami Beach, FL 33139, USA

telephone (1) 305 604 50 00 or (1) 800 OUTPOST   **fax** (1) 305 604 51 80

room rates from US$350 (suites from US$1,000)

four seasons

Armani, Prada, Gucci, Versace, Etro, Dolce & Gabbana … reformed shoppers beware! For you this may be the most dangerous hotel location on earth. Housed in a fifteenth-century Renaissance convent, in the midst of what is known as Milan's 'golden triangle', the Four Seasons is surrounded by all the great names in fashion. This strategic position has proved irresistible to serious shoppers, not to mention the small army of models, agents, editors, buyers and photographers wanting to be part of the splendid design and cosmopolitan atmosphere that is so essentially Milanese.

In reality most of Milan is not like this at all. This is a tough, gritty, industrial city – the engine that drives Italy's economy. As the old saying goes, *Milano lavora e Roma mangia* – the Milanese work, the Romans eat. The mentality of Milan is that of a northern European city. And it is certainly not, with the exception of the old inner city, very pretty. True, it has La Scala and the Duomo, but in general, as a visiting *New York Times* critic so aptly summed it up, 'the city is so grey it makes me want to take it to a carwash'.

Via Gesù no. 8 is a retreat from the grey. Nestled in the city's small but charming medieval core on a quiet street of pale-pink and yellow stately palazzi, Four Seasons envelops its guests in a cocoon of quiet sophistication and restrained beauty. And though this may seem at odds with the city, it is, in reality, a very Milanese phenomenon. If Rome is the 'eternal' city then Milan, the locals will tell you, is the 'internal' city. Everything goes on behind closed doors. Milan's secrets, they say, lie in its courtyards; and the courtyard behind the restrained buttermilk facade of this former palazzo had quite a secret of its own. Acquired in 1987, the property was under extensive reconstruction when first the granite columns, then the vaulted ceilings and eventually the remnants of Flemish-inspired frescoes were uncovered, all belonging to a Renaissance convent. The building had been modernized so often over the centuries that the fifteenth-century convent of Santa Maria del Gesù, to which the street owes its name, was completely buried and forgotten.

As a direct result of this discovery, architect Carlo Meda abandoned his original plans and instead redesigned the hotel to resurrect the architecture of the cloister. The elegant columns that now grace the beautifully restored courtyard give no hint of the sophisticated technology that made all this possible.

Surrounding a magnificent courtyard, the Four Seasons Milan is a haven of peace and quiet in a bustling city

Gilded filigree in the first-floor lift hall is typical of the stylish approach to decoration

Details of the design scheme resemble the early work of Milan's master architect Gio Ponti

Architect Carlo Meda's design revolved entirely around the restoration of the recently rediscovered convent

The colonnaded glory of the original fifteenth-century cloister emerged during excavation of the site

Gilded mirrors and ecclesiastical candlesticks contrast with the simple, modern tones of the lobby

The restaurant, Il Teatro, has become a local favourite. Giorgio Armani is one of many famous regulars

An ornate palazzo ceiling distinguishes Jil Sander's favourite first-floor courtyard room

La Colonna, the less formal café-restaurant, serves Milanese cuisine (with particular focus on desserts)

A corner of the original priory
is now an area designated for
card games

The ground-floor suites retain
the original fifteenth-century
vaulted ceilings

Carefully selected antiques abound,
but the interior never threatens to
become fussy or over-decorated

The library, one of the few public spaces
to retain the original architecture, is
popular for afternoon tea

Unusual detail adorns the hotel's
corridors, such as these remnants
of decorative lace ironwork

Carefully, painstakingly, centuries
of paint were stripped away to reveal
remnants of sixteenth-century frescoes

The seductively shaped oval staircase is
another reminder of Ponti's particular
take on modernist aesthetics

Amenities such as a fully equipped
gymnasium are housed in a large
underground area

By placing utilities like kitchens below
ground, the original courtyard spaces
could be dedicated to guest rooms

A complex, hidden steel skeleton was introduced to provide structural stability because the original columns could not possibly have carried the load of two floors, while most of the space given over to utilitarian areas such as kitchens, offices, conference rooms and storage is located below ground so as not to compromise the dimensions of the above-ground cloister. As a result, many of the guest rooms were able to retain the magnificent vaulted ceilings of the original fifteenth-century architecture.

But it is not just the good fortune of uncovering a historical jewel that makes this one of the most rewarding hotel experiences in Europe. In a city where the locals are not much partial to visiting hotel lobbies, this refined address on Via Gesù has become an accepted part of Milan's inner scene. La Veranda, the café, is a favourite lunch and aperitif spot among Milan's fashion and banking set, and Il Teatro, presided over by award-winning chef Sergio Mei, is favoured by local luminaries such as Riccardo Muti, conductor at La Scala, and Giorgio Armani – no doubt because of dishes such as *risotto mantecato con mazzacolle e carciofi alla mentuccia* (imperial prawn risotto with artichokes and peppermint).

If food is a big attraction at Four Seasons, so too is the design. Crisp white walls accented by the odd remnant of a fresco, parquet and terrazzo floors, a beautifully sculptural oval staircase, and Cassina furniture create an atmosphere that recalls the elegant modernism of Gio Ponti, Italy's most celebrated twentieth-century architect. Interestingly, designer Pamela Babey opted *not* to cater to the building's pedigree. There is a total lack of reproduction furniture, heavy fabrics or plush. Instead, modern Italian design is juxtaposed very successfully with the character and charm of the surviving Renaissance architecture. Judging by the sheer volume of shopping bags scattered about the foyer, the only thing it hasn't been able to supply is willpower.

address Four Seasons, Via Gesù 8, 20121 Milan, Italy

telephone (39) 2 770 88 **fax** (39) 2 770 85 000

room rates from L666,000 (suites from L995,000)

soho grand hotel

When it opened in 1996, the SoHo Grand was the first new hotel in SoHo for over a century. This world-famous area of Manhattan, home to the greatest collection of cast-iron architecture in the US, has long resisted any attempt to alter its precious architectural heritage. No wonder then that plans for the SoHo Grand, a structure large enough to house almost four hundred rooms and rising to fifteen storeys (in an area where five or six is the norm), initially met with vigorous local resistance. Yet the inescapable fact is that SoHo really needs a hotel (or two). The area has become vital not just to sections of the art, photographic, design and publishing industries, but also, thanks to the close proximity of New York University, to the academic world too. And anyone who has ever taken a taxi to get to an appointment in SoHo from mid- or uptown hotels will know that arriving on time is about as dependable as getting a cab driver who speaks English.

Unfazed by local objections, proprietor Emanuel Stern took a constructive attitude towards the obstacle of local disapproval. He readily acknowledges that artists are the ones who come in and make an area attractive, while businessmen merely follow in their wake to capitalize on that. So to ensure that his approach was not seen as exploitative Stern made the smart commitment to root the hotel as much in the local community as possible. In practice this meant employing a SoHo-based designer, working with SoHo-based artists and galleries, and drawing from the SoHo vernacular for the internal as well as the external architecture of the hotel. Stern interviewed fourteen designers before settling on William Sofield, ex-partner in SoHo's trend-setting Aero design studios.

Sofield, whose former work includes creating many of the famously seductive room settings for Ralph Lauren Home, approached this project by blending the area's industrial background with the rich vocabulary of the local architecture. SoHo's famous loft buildings feature Victorian, Italianate, oriental and even Egyptian-inspired embellishment and detailing. Thus the Egyptian columns, oriental lanterns and turn-of-the-century Arts and Crafts ornament that distinguish the SoHo Grand's interior have a secure local precedent.

But it may well have been the constraints placed on Sofield that inspired the true originality and creativity of his scheme. For a host of restrictions was put in the hotel's way.

The ground floor of the SoHo Grand is a raw, muscular space that could double as a set for *Batman*

Vintage Manhattan photography decorates the rooms and is also available for purchase

The pared-down lobby evokes the feeling of America's grand turn-of-the-century railway stations

Arts-and-Crafts-style furniture reflects designer William Sofield's history-conscious approach

The Canal House restaurant, a tall and impressive yet cosy space, specializes in classic American dishes

Despite the scrupulous attention to period detail, there is also a state-of-the-art fitness centre

According to city ordinance, for instance, the ground floor was prohibited from housing any traditional hotel functions because the area is, by legal definition, a flood plain – even though the swamp that prompted this legislation was filled in a century ago. Thus the entrance is quite out of the ordinary, a bit like arriving in a subway station. An empty cavern dominated by immense brick columns and a staircase made of steel girders, this brutalist space serves as an anteroom to the main lobby and reception one floor above. It heightens the impact not just of the lobby, but also of the staircase, embedded with the glass-bottle bottoms traditionally used along the inner edge of sidewalks in the area to illuminate the basements below. It also completely disguises the fact that the ground floor was not allowed to be used as a reception. The design is gutsy, industrial and artistic, an apt metaphor for SoHo itself.

The lobby, an area of appropriately grand proportions, is divided in half by a row of Egyptian-style columns that march across the space in military fashion. One side is strictly business (checking in, checking out, picking up messages), the other (further divided into salon, bar and restaurant) strictly pleasure. With its magnificently high ceilings and monumental proportions (the biggest lamp shades you've ever seen), the restaurant prompted one New York newspaper critic to liken the experience to 'dining in Stalinist Russia'.

Except the food is probably a lot better. In the tradition of many Hip Hotels, the two-star Canal House restaurant is a big drawcard in its own right. Rated by the *New York Times* as 'American food for the knowing diner', its reinvented American classics include Manhattan clam chowder, crab Louis (crab meat with slices of avocado and pink grapefruit), and grilled lamb tenderloin with spoon bread. The atmosphere is cool and calm, a marked departure from the clamour of the SoHo scene – so seductive, in fact, that even the locals who once opposed the hotel so vigorously now regularly drop in for lunch.

address SoHo Grand Hotel, 310 West Broadway, New York, NY 10013, USA

telephone (1) 212 965 30 00   **fax** (1) 212 965 32 00

room rates from US$239 (suites from US$1,049)

four seasons hotel

In the 1920s, when the US skyscraper boom began in earnest, impossibly tall buildings symbolized the country's mood. The Chrysler Building, Rockefeller Center and the Empire State Building rose as monuments to human ingenuity and energy. These cathedrals of commerce were not only uniquely American – irrefutable proof of America's world leadership in engineering – they were also paragons of promise. Even today, no one could visit New York and fail to be impressed by the skyline. The overwhelming optimism and conviction expressed by the sheer scale and craftsmanship of Manhattan's skyscrapers, particularly the elegant Art Deco originals, remain utterly compelling. In the words of Nathan Silver, author of *Lost New York*, 'an encounter with magnificent architecture irradiates even someone alienated and disaffected'. History, 'the lamp of memory', illuminates these buildings, evoking for each new generation the impressive confidence of a past age.

The 'lamp of memory' is certainly a tool that I.M. Pei makes use of in his architecture, and to dramatic effect. Just as his famous glass pyramid in the courtyard of the Louvre in Paris evokes Napoleon's fascination with ancient Egypt, I.M. Pei's design for the Four Seasons Hotel evokes heroic New York – the days when the glamour, confidence and sheer craftsmanship of the American skyscraper symbolized America's world dominance in engineering and were a testament to the overwhelming success of capitalism.

I.M. Pei seems to understand very well the irresistibility of buildings imbued with history. For that is the power of the Four Seasons. Walk into the lobby, with its massive bronze urns, intricate marble floor and spectacular onyx ceiling soaring ten metres above the entrance hall, and you are instantly transported back to the glamour and prosperity of the twenties. With this new skyscraper – which at fifty-two floors is the tallest hotel in New York – he has truly captured the original magic of Manhattan. And in reinventing the classic American skyscraper he has observed the tradition of quality as well as scale. This is a building that makes no attempt to hide its intention to impress, but it does so through the timeless qualities of monumental scale and superb craftsmanship. The confidence communicated by its architecture is certainly infectious. No wonder the Four Seasons Hotel is so consistently popular, and with locals as well as out-of-towners.

Gigantic urns at the Four Seasons
Hotel recall the grand scale and
design of Manhattan Art Deco

Beneath a monumental porthole, New
Yorkers gather every evening for a drink
and a chat in the restaurant anteroom

The orchid suggests health and fitness –
preferable to a photo of the gym (which
is large but not very photogenic)

The soaring space of the lobby was
inspired by the golden age of
the American skyscraper

A Hollywood version of Manhattan –
this perhaps best sums up the style
of the guest rooms

The Bar is also a popular meeting spot
with locals, a very good sign in
ultra-critical New York

At 110 square metres, each of the
eighteen deluxe suites is larger than
the average Manhattan apartment

Restrained glitz: restaurant Fifty Seven
Fifty Seven recalls the pared-down
glamour of American Art Deco

The tallest hotel in Manhattan, the
Four Seasons offers tantalizing
views of the city

Furniture was commissioned to
capture the optimistic spirit
of the Art Deco twenties

The restaurant, Fifty Seven Fifty Seven,
was recently awarded three stars by
the *New York Times*

A typical view includes the Empire State
Building, one of Manhattan's most
famous Art Deco skyscrapers

The lobby is divided into two immense
areas: grand foyer and the terraced
lounge that wraps around it

The corner rooms offer big windows,
lots of light and superb views of
Manhattan's impressive architecture

The interior was by Chhada, Siembieda
& Partners, the design group responsible
for Asia's superb Regent hotels

In a minimal palette of neutral tones,
the interior pays tribute to legendary
French designer Jean-Michel Frank

Only by including people can
a photograph convey the scale of
these sleek monuments to New York

Symmetry, precision and a sense of
theatre: these are the qualities I.M. Pei
has given the Four Seasons Hotel

'Noo Yawkers' are infamous as the most critical audience in the world, so it is a real testament to this hotel that they flock to meet in its bar for drinks (the Four Seasons' 'French martini' and 'citrus martini' lead the field), to sample the cuisine in the Fifty Seven Fifty Seven Restaurant (awarded a three-star rating from the *New York Times*, unprecedented for a hotel dining room) and to meet friends for a quick pre-theatre supper in the Lobby Restaurant. In the morning they will even stand in line for a breakfast table. Taste the lemon and ricotta hotcakes and you'll understand why. In short, the Four Seasons has become something of a hangout, and not just for chief executives and producer types slavishly accustomed to the immaculate level of service and impressive standard of food, but also for locals who work in the neighbourhood and for the film stars who like to linger in the lobby waiting to protest at being recognized.

Then there are the guest rooms straight out of those old black-and-white movies set in swanky Manhattan, where men are always in black tie, and impossibly elegant women in long glittering dresses drape themselves around handsome interiors. Double the size of the average New York hotel room, they have sweeping views of the sparkling city below, showing New York exactly the way you always imagined it to be: big, glamorous and impressive. Some even have their own terrace, which, particularly on the upper floors, can be quite something. Yet large and luxurious as they are, they are not overdone. Care was taken to emulate the stylistic atmosphere of American Art Deco without merely reconstructing the past. A very contemporary clarity and simplicity, in sophisticated shades of sand and bronze, is what you get at the Four Seasons New York.

So is the Four Seasons Hotel more expensive because of all this glamour, luxury and space? Who cares? As one prominent New York travel agent observed, 'The Four Seasons is like a Broadway hit. Everyone wants to go. No matter what the price.'

address Four Seasons Hotel, 57 East 57 Street, New York, NY 10022, USA
telephone (1) 212 758 57 00 **fax** (1) 212 758 57 11
room rates from US$515 (suites from US$1050)

the mercer

Almost a decade ago André Balazs, hotel and nightclub impresario and proprietor of LA's Chateau Marmont, acquired an imposing red-brick building on the corner of Spring and Mercer Streets in the heart of trendy SoHo and announced plans to open a hotel. Much delayed and postponed, its opening became the most eagerly anticipated event in Manhattan. The big question, of course, is was it worth the wait? The answer is an unequivocal yes. Why? Because it is entirely unlike any other hotel in New York, if not the world.

By preserving the windows, the ceiling height and the proportions of the warehouse space, the Mercer is the first hotel to offer a taste of 'loft living', an urban signature that is completely original to New York. The conventional notion of a hotel room has been abandoned. Instead every room feels like a loft, with the seductive qualities of unencumbered space and abundant natural light – exactly what attracted the community of artists who first gave this area its distinctive character.

The only problem with a loft space is how to furnish it. A loft demands a design approach that enhances rather than fills the space. That is why Balazs chose to work with Parisian designer Christian Liaigre. His combination of handsome, pared-down furniture in African Wenge wood, neutrally toned textiles, simple lamps, dark wooden floors, pure white walls, crisp white linen, and a hint of lilac leather on elegant banquettes is exactly what was needed – a subtle, clean and classic approach that steers clear of furniture fashion and design clichés.

The design commitment to the loft experience is absolute, and continues with the bathrooms. The Mercer has the best bathrooms in North America. Period. This is not just because they're all white marble and white mosaic tile or because they're incredibly spacious, with a centrally placed bath and a stylish stainless-steel trolley for towels and cosmetics. It is because they are so cleverly integrated into the overall space. What, after all, is the point of going to great lengths (not to mention expense) to preserve the integrity of a warehouse loft space if the bathroom is then relegated to a pokey little cubicle? At the Mercer the bathrooms are open to, and part of, the overall interior. Although there are folding doors to provide privacy and partition when so required, why use them when taking a bath in full view of the surrounding space and the buildings across the street is such a seductive highlight – so urban, so decadent, so SoHo?

Almost like a Pop Art installation, the
end of each corridor is defined
by a different colour

In the Mercer's startlingly white
bathrooms, the simplest touch
of colour stands out

The restrained yet dramatic use of
colour in the corridors mimics
that in the rooms

A massive square bath illuminated
by an overhead light well is typical
of the top-floor bathrooms

Colour is used sparingly, like jewelry –
just enough for effect. Even the hues
are reminiscent of pale gemstones

Large, white, spacious and refined, the
Mercer has what many critics agree
are the best bathrooms in the US

A corner room with Liaigre-designed
chairs and the Mercer's trademark
oval conversation table

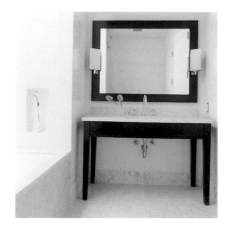

African Wenge wood, Carrara marble
surfaces and white walls are Christian
Liaigre's signature ingredients

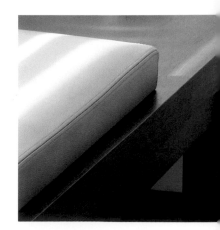

Slim banquettes upholstered in lilac
leather are an elegant touch
in the all-white interiors

Wherever possible, the cast-iron pillars of the nineteenth-century warehouse building were left in position

Instead of the usual desk that nobody uses, Liaigre provided each and every room with a generous oval table

Every detail, even the wall-mounted bedside lamp, was custom-made for the Mercer

Pale green and lilac are perfect colours to complement the clean white of this uncompromisingly urban environment

The beds are immaculate, with neutral-shaded linen covers and Frette sheets. Who wants to rough it in a loft?

Dark African Wenge wood contrasts with modern bone china and orange raffia place mats

All the rooms, even the smallest, have that distinctly urban feeling of a loft space

Daylight is what makes SoHo so special – it is the only area of Manhattan without (sun-blocking) skyscrapers

The stainless-steel trolley equipped with towels and cosmetics is standard to all Mercer bathrooms

SoHo (*South of Houston* Street) is unique in Manhattan because it's the only area without skyscrapers. The tallest buildings are a modest six storeys, allowing daylight to filter in and so avoiding the dark canyons that dominate the rest of New York City. Once upon a time these light-filled warehouses, with their acres of space, were inhabited almost exclusively by industry. Then, after a period of neglect and abandonment, they were discovered by artists, who moved in and transformed the buildings and the area too. Now it's a different story. The last couple of decades have seen the price of a SoHo loft pull just about even with the price of an Upper East Side apartment. Struggling artists can definitely no longer afford to live here. Yet though much vilified (particularly by the art community) this gentrification of SoHo has helped create the environment that now sustains some of Manhattan's best boutiques, restaurants and bars.

Despite the competition, Balazs has boldly thrown his hat into the ring. The Mercer Kitchen, a restaurant located in the basement of the building, creates the feel of eating in the kitchen, 'always the best setting for conversation among the best of friends' according to Balazs. Illuminated by glass bottle-bottoms embedded in the sidewalk overhead (very characteristic of the area), the ambience combined with the cuisine of chef Jean-Georges Vongerichten has made The Mercer Kitchen one of the most consistently popular and fashionable restaurants in SoHo.

The matt-black crowd of ad agency staff, art directors, photographers and fashion people may have shunted out the artists, but SoHo still has an attitude and an atmosphere you won't find with the 'big coat, small poodle' crowd on the Upper East Side. For Nathan Silver, author of *Lost New York*, 'if anything should stand forever as a radiant image of the essential New York, it ought to be these [SoHo's] commercial buildings.' Continually evolving in response to contemporary needs, they are 'the best and purest that New York has to offer.'

---

address The Mercer, 147 Mercer Street, New York, NY 10012, USA

telephone (1) 212 966 60 60 **fax** (1) 212 965 38 38

room rates from US$350 (suites from US$925)

hôtel costes

Jean Louis Costes is no shrinking violet. In the early eighties he set all of Paris talking by opening a new café – a café that broke all the rules. It had no chandeliers, no mirrors, no fancy Belle Epoque embellishment and no address worth mentioning. Situated on the corner of the distinctly unfashionable rue St-Denis, near Les Halles (an area better known for its ladies of the night), and designed by a then complete unknown (a former art director at Christian Dior named Philippe Starck), Café Costes nevertheless became a huge hit. It was *the* place in Paris. The men's toilet became just about the most photographed space in the history of interior design, Italian furniture manufacturer Driade sold almost a million of the café's trademark 'Costes chairs', and Philippe Starck became something of a national hero.

Almost twenty years later Jean Louis Costes has done it again. Everyone is talking about Hôtel Costes and its *wunderkind* designer Jacques Garcia. Situated on the ultra chichi rue St-Honoré, this is the place where all of Paris is having lunch. Ditto dinner. Even other hotels send their guests here. It is *the* place to go for pre-dinner *apéritifs* or after-dinner *digestifs*. It is where public relations firms arrange press interviews for their celebrity clients. It's a scene … and a circus. But what a circus! Hôtel Costes rekindles the exaggerated styles and atmosphere of France's Second Empire. History meets fantasy in eccentrically decorated spaces that surround a courtyard straight out of an aristocrat's palazzo. A small, dark, intimate dining room created in a style best described as 'oriental opium den' is next to the 'Herbarium', a perfect lunchtime retreat decorated wall to wall with mounted and framed pharmacological leaves. Yet another dining room is in the exaggerated neoclassical style of the late nineteenth century. For winter days there's a cosy space isolated by thick curtains arranged around a monumental fantasy of a fireplace, as well as the opportunity to dine in the glass-enclosed corridors surrounding the courtyard like a circular greenhouse.

This powerful mix of texture, colour, pattern and historic period is the speciality and the passion of interior designer Jacques Garcia. Neoclassicism, orientalism, Empire Revival: these are his decorative hallmarks – preferably mixed. His love of excess is in evidence throughout the hotel: in the corridors, the guest suites, the bathrooms.

A magnificent Belle Epoque fireplace warms one of the winter dining rooms of Hôtel Costes

Bathroom floors in richly coloured, ornate tiles satisfy designer Jacques Garcia's penchant for orientalism

In the lobby you feel as if you are waiting for a train in an Agatha Christie novel

No detail has been overlooked: the classical statues were cast in modern plastic and painted to appear old

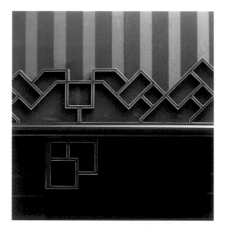

Garcia is a master at mixing texture, pattern and colour, particularly if they have historic precedents

The light-filled corridor that runs along the courtyard is used for winter lunches

Pattern on pattern on pattern – Garcia's approach creates a luxurious atmosphere

Fifties chairs straight out of *La Dolce Vita* create a certain Latin ambience on the terrace of the hotel's courtyard

The reception desk, where guests can sit down to check in, is in the ornate style of the Belle Epoque

The bathrooms are the only reminder that this is the twentieth century – but then only in terms of plumbing, not style

The stools that furnish the Chinese-opium-den-inspired bar are typical of Jacques Garcia's attention to detail

The courtyard is like that of an old Tuscan palazzo belonging to an eccentric Italian count

Garcia designed the furniture himself. These turn-of-the-century salon chairs feature in different fabrics and colours

A popular spot for afternoon tea, the Herbarium is decorated with framed pharmacological specimens

Designer Jacques Garcia is opposed to the trend towards simplicity; he prefers the more seductive quality of complexity

Hidden in the catacombs, the gym has every machine and gadget any gym junkie could dream of

Mirrors, flower paintings and a chinoiserie trellis frame the door leading into the opium-den bar

A neoclassically inspired room decorated with Egyptian Revivalist touches is one of six ground-floor restaurant spaces

Even the amazing subterranean pool, buried in the catacombs, does not escape his talent for staging drama and fantasy. 'Why,' jokes Garcia, 'do things simply, when you can make them more complicated?'

All the decorative Belle Epoque details, so scrupulously omitted from Café Costes, are reintroduced with abandon in Hôtel Costes. No trace of Monsieur Starck here. Jean Louis Costes clearly demands originality, even if that means reinventing the past. If everyone else is going modern, he seems to be saying, I'll go antique. Thus the unexpected choice of Jacques Garcia as designer. Previously known only to the most exclusive circles of super-rich French society, Garcia is the man who uses his encyclopaedic knowledge of the decorative arts to create period environments more fantastic than they perhaps ever were. As journalist Philippe Seulliet explained in a recent profile, 'he creates rooms which seem to bear the traces of generations but are, in fact, the product of his inspired and gently irreverent imagination.'

Extensively published in the more rarefied interiors magazines, his best-known projects such as Château Champ de Bataille in Normandy have, in the main, been for himself. Hôtel Costes was an opportunity to give his distinct signature a more commercial and populist expression. To create its sensual, multilayered, tapestry-like environment, Garcia commissioned all the lamps, furniture, fabrics, wallpaper and floor coverings to be custom-made. With the exception of some fabrics and wallpapers produced by a small, highly specialized English firm, there is nothing in Hôtel Costes that can be purchased in a shop. That is one reason why the result is so striking. Garcia has taken a style that had been generally regarded as pure personal indulgence, even folly, and translated it to the pragmatic and unforgiving world of commercial design. The result is a great success, betraying no sign of compromise or unsuitability.

So, forget the Bauhaus dictum 'less is more'. Start thinking 'too much is never enough'.

---

address Hôtel Costes, 239 rue St-Honoré, 75001 Paris, France

telephone (33) 1 4244 5000 **fax** (33) 1 4244 5001

room rates from 1,750 FFr (suites from 3,250 FFr)

l'hôtel

It was in this hotel, on an impossibly narrow street in the middle of the art and antique neighbourhood of the Left Bank, that Oscar Wilde penned the tragicomic line 'I'm dying beyond my means', in what proved to be one of his last letters. Even on his deathbed, his health and his finances in a perilous state, Wilde didn't lose the sardonic wit that was to make him a literary legend.

Today, this same address on the rue des Beaux-Arts is still operating as a hotel and it is doing its best to live up to its legacy. Predictably, one room is dedicated to Wilde's memory (he really did die here): a vaguely Victorian, slightly shabby, cluttered room furnished with a big sleigh bed and decorated with Wilde's framed letters. I doubt Wilde would have been impressed by the Oscar Wilde Suite. Nor would he have fancied the room-key medallions featuring his bust. But what he would have *loved*, I'm sure, is room 34, which is entirely covered (walls, bedspread, furniture) in *faux* leopard skin.

I first heard about L'Hôtel more than a decade ago from friends in the art world. 'It's a crazy place,' they said, 'you'll love it, the rooms are completely over the top'. But exactly what did that mean? 'Never mind, you'll see, just ask

to stay in different rooms'. And so I did. My first room was all red. Red velour curtains, red carpet, a red velvet bedspread with red satin trim, accented with a scattering of black and gold-leaf Empire antiques. The bathroom, in contrast, was all green marble. The style was 'mini-Napoleon'. Normally I would expect such a combination to make me claustrophobic, but presented in Parisian proportions, against high ceilings and beautiful windows, it was surprisingly cosy and elegant. My second room (later the same week) was all green: a chartreuse green carpet, dark emerald green velour curtains and green velvet bedspread contrasted with antique chairs, cupboards and cabinets painted ivory white, and a cream marble bathroom. There are also rooms with silver and chocolate-brown psychedelic wallpaper; a red, white and blue 'thirties' tribute to Marilyn Monroe (strange considering she was a star in the fifties); and a flower-power, Laura-Ashley-on-acid penthouse suite. Needless to say, every room at L'Hôtel is different, each a potent decorative excursion.

Architecturally speaking, the highlight of the hotel is the staircase well, a round neoclassical tower decorated with plaster medallions which rises from a star-patterned terrazzo floor towards a clear dome open to the sky. There is absolutely nothing else like it in Paris, yet it is the kind of *folie* that is completely at home here, particularly at an address like rue des Beaux-Arts. This is the heart of the Left Bank, the very centre of the Paris of Ernest Hemingway, Pablo Picasso, Gertrude Stein, Man Ray, F. Scott Fitzgerald and innumerable other legendary artists and writers. Just walking the streets is pure entertainment. There are beautiful little specialized shops selling old books and rare artifacts; small galleries that insist on 'big' openings that inevitably spill out onto the stone-cobbled streets; and the odd shop with a minimalist display that shows off the latest in fashion or interior decoration. For window shopping, for sitting in cafés and watching life go by, for squeezing the most out of what the Left Bank has to offer, there is not a better location in Paris.

If you're the type that occasionally likes to stay in, order room service, or hang around the lobby, then this place is not for you. There is no room service and no lobby. There used to be a funky bar in the catacombs under the building but that closed and the hotel restaurant has the forlorn feeling of a set from *Last Tango in Paris*. L'Hôtel is really about the rooms and the location; it is definitely a place for people who like to strike out on their own and for aesthetes who appreciate the unconventional.

Ironically – perhaps appropriately – the very Parisian feeling of L'Hôtel owes to the efforts of an American. The exotic decor and the extraordinary staircase tower were created in the sixties by the American decorator Robin Westbrook. At the time it must have been streets ahead of all the other hotels in Paris. In many ways it still is. The attraction is still as potent as ever, perhaps even more so because nothing has changed. Where else can you follow in Oscar Wilde's decadent footsteps *and* enjoy staying in a series of genuine sixties interiors?

address L'Hôtel, 13 rue des Beaux-Arts, 75006 Paris, France
telephone (33) 1 4441 9900 **fax** (33) 1 4325 6481
room rates from 1,000 FFr (suites from 2,800 FFr)

hotel lancaster

'Grown-up glamour' is how Grace Leo-Andrieu likes to describe her hotel. It's hard to disagree. Hotel Lancaster may well be the most glamorous hotel in Paris. Not because it dazzles you with glitz – it's too discreet for that. This is not the Ritz. It doesn't employ a small army of uniformed staff and there is no 'scene' in the lobby. But that is exactly the point. The Lancaster, as Leo-Andrieu sees it, is for people who have nothing left to prove. If you're past impressing people with where you are staying, then you're ready for the more subtle pleasures of a hotel that US *Town & Country* magazine recently described as 'the most sophisticated, refined hotel experience in Paris'.

The understated luxury and timeless quality of the Lancaster have long been attracting international celebrities, including Cary Grant, Grace Kelly and Clark Gable. Marlene Dietrich virtually made this her Paris home: one of the suites is named after her and decorated entirely in her favourite colour, lilac. Yet despite its high-profile clientele, the Lancaster has always been very low profile, and Leo-Andrieu intends to keep it that way. Quite simply, the hotel is for hotel guests only. The dining room, for example – idyllically situated overlooking a splendid courtyard garden – is

not open to the public. Period. Hotel Lancaster consequently feels more like a club than a hotel. Here, as a guest, you are free to entertain, drink or dine without the rest of the world watching and without having to compete with them for a table booking.

Private and beautifully decorated, the Lancaster has a style all its own. The first proprietor to convert this grand Haussmann-era apartment building (four floors, four apartments) into a hotel was Emile Wolf, a Swiss gentleman with a rather fine eye who was helped in his treasure hunt for the hotel by the fact that his housekeeper's father was an antique dealer. Endless visits to Paris auctions, antique stalls and flea markets brought superb Baccarat crystal, tapestries, Louis XV and XVI chairs and countless other fine pieces to the hotel. M. Wolf, it seems, was also something of a clock aficionado and today every other room features a piece from his remarkable collection. The same is true of the work of the Russian court portraitist Boris Pastoukhoff, a White Russian who was forced into exile by the revolution and ended up in Paris. During the twenties and early thirties Pastoukhoff would often make the Lancaster his home, using his talent to pay his way.

Some of the bathrooms of Hotel
Lancaster were restored to recreate
the glamorous twenties originals

The bar: vintage champagne,
avant-garde photography books,
and a Thai silk lamp

The porte-cochère of this Haussmann-
era apartment building is now an
elegantly minimal entrance

The original proprietor, Monsieur Emile Wolf, had a passion for collecting clocks

The Dietrich Suite is entirely decorated in shades of Marlene's favourite colour, lilac

The courtyard garden was completely redesigned in a more modern, more exotic, eastern style

As a result the hotel ended up owning nearly eighty oil paintings by an artist whose work is also to be found in the permanent collections of top museums around the world, including the Brooklyn Museum of Fine Arts and the Museo Reina Sofia in Madrid.

Emile Wolf certainly left behind an impressive legacy, but by the time Grace Leo-Andrieu purchased the property in 1996 the hotel was in dire need of modernization. A panel of respected experts was consulted as to how best to restore the antiques, and the priceless pieces were carefully repaired. Old, tired upholstery was replaced by plain silks in oriental tones of mauve, lilac, pink and ochre. Contemporary pieces by designers such as Christian Liaigre were introduced, as were collections of chinoiserie coffee tables, Japanese lacquered nests of tables, cachepots of orchids, celadon bowls and specially commissioned Chinese ink portraits in the dining room. The result is the most seductive kind of environment of all – a mix of the modern, the antique and the oriental. It's an exotic blend – just like its owner. Grace Leo-Andrieu made her name in the world of hotels with highly individual, cosmopolitan places like the Guanahani in St Barts, the Clarence in Dublin and the Paris Left Bank Hotel Montalembert. Born in Hong Kong (to hotelier parents), educated in the United States, and married to a Frenchman, Leo-Andrieu translated her mixed cultural experiences into one of the most exciting hotels to open in Paris in the nineties. But what she created is not only different, it is also very professional, and nothing less than traditional in its standards of service.

Grace Leo-Andrieu remembers when, fresh out of Cornell Hotel School, she was working at the Warwick Hotel just next door. Every time she walked past the sleepy Lancaster with its doorman lazily smoking out front she would imagine all the things she would do 'if I could get my hands on that place'. A decade later she did.

---

address Hotel Lancaster, 7 rue de Berri, 75008 Paris, France

telephone (33) 1 4076 4076 **fax** (33) 1 4076 4000

room rates from 1,650 FFr (suites from 4,050 FFr)

hotel montalembert

In a city that boasts as many hotels as Paris, it is difficult to believe that until recently the choice was rather limited. You could live it up in grand Right Bank style (if you could afford it) or settle for the cosy, quaint charms of the Left Bank – exposed beams, low ceilings and minuscule bathrooms (if at all). Aristocrats and powerbrokers stayed grand; tourists stayed quaint. It worked rather well. But then a new breed of traveller started to appear: the frequent flyer, a thoroughly modern professional with thoroughly modern needs. The Montalembert was the first hotel to cater specifically to this new type – without sacrificing the personality of Paris.

Situated on the rue Montalembert – named after the comte de Montalembert, the great nineteenth-century writer and orator – this historic limestone landmark was built in 1926. Located just off the boulevard Saint-Germain, a quick stroll from the famous Café Deux Magots and Café Flore, the Montalembert has been a favourite with artists and writers since its inception. Yet by the time the property was acquired in 1990 by Grace Leo-Andrieu and her husband Stephane, the hotel was so much on the decline that it looked more like a fusty, nondescript government building. After a nine-

month, eight-million dollar restoration, Hotel Montalembert reopened under the direction of Leo-Andrieu's pace-setting hotel company, with, as Christian Liaigre puts it, 'the soul it never had'. It also opened just in time, noted *Gourmet* magazine, 'to take up the slack left by the demise of the much-loved Hotel Pont Royal', whose bar had been a literary Mecca, frequented by the area's publishers and authors.

The goal of the Montalembert renovation was simple: to integrate a distinct, contemporary style with the elegant original architecture of the building. The hotel's collection of antique pieces was restored; Liaigre's furniture designs were installed throughout the fifty-one rooms and five suites; and sculptor Eric Schmitt was commissioned to produce the 'neo-barbaric' bronze wall lights. But the greatest success of the Montalembert's reinvention has to be the ground-floor space. A café, restaurant, cosy library and bar were eked out of an area not much bigger than a small apartment. This is no mere breakfast nook for hotel guests, but a fully functional series of independent spaces. Defined not by partitions, which would have turned the area into a rabbit warren, but by different levels of light intensity, these spaces have become an authentic Left Bank hangout.

The Montalembert's restaurant has become a popular lunch-time haunt for the neighbourhood's *antiquaires* and *littérateurs*. The food is like the design – a mix of the modern and the classic. New cuisine includes salmon with fresh herbs and sautéed chicken in sherry vinegar with braised courgettes, while French classics include *lapin à la moutarde à l'ancien*. In the winter the fireside book-lined space adjoining the restaurant is a perfect, and popular, spot for afternoon tea, served from an impressive array of tisanes by the city's best tea purveyors, Mariage Frères. And in summer the bamboo of the small garden adjoining the library beckons for early evening aperitifs.

Designer Christian Liaigre is no longer so enamoured with the eye-catching marine and taupe rug depicting the count's handwriting that paves the way into the hotel, but the Montalembert has certainly not lost any of the appeal that made it *le must de Paris* in the early nineties. In fact this hotel is a convincing argument for the wisdom of Grace Leo-Andrieu's signature approach of adhering to a simple palette of unpretentious luxury. From the oak floors to the Italian marble in the bathrooms, from the monogrammed Frette linen to the flowers by Christian Tortu (the most stylish florist in Paris), every detail reflects her commitment to a consistent but contemporary sense of quality. Guests have a choice between traditional with a hint of modern (refurbished Louis Philippe antiques with the odd modern lamp and Liaigre chair) or completely modern rooms furnished in the solid sycamore timber designs that typify Liaigre's measured minimalism.

Steeped in Left Bank culture, the Montalembert feels like the Paris from a book. And that is because it is: in Nancy Mitford's *The Pursuit of Love* the Montalembert is the romantic 'secret' tucked off the boulevard St-Germain; and in Peter Mayle's novel *Chasing Cézanne* it is the epitome of chic, the logical place for the hero, a photographer for glossy magazines, to hide out.

address Hotel Montalembert, 3 rue de Montalembert, 75007 Paris, France
telephone (33) 1 4549 6868 **fax** (33) 1 4549 6949
room rates from 1,675 FFr (suites from 2,830 FFr)

the governor hotel

It's hard to say which is more of a surprise, the city or the hotel. Portland is one of those 'best kept secret' type of cities. It is small enough to have preserved a sense of intimacy and familiarity, but large enough (with a population of around a million) to support the kind of infrastructure that keeps life interesting – shops, theatres, cinemas, museums, restaurants and bars. And just outside the city there is a countryside still as majestic and unspoiled as when it was first encountered by explorers Meriwether Lewis and William Clark almost two hundred years ago.

It was news of a stately old hotel with vast murals and funky furniture inspired by the exploits of these two legendary American pioneers that brought me to Portland in the first place. The extraordinary interior of the Governor Hotel (built in 1909) celebrates the Lewis and Clark expedition to the American Northwest in 1804–6, for which they travelled two thousand miles across the United States, charting new territories and recording their meetings with previously unencountered Native American tribes such as the Nez Perce Indians. Appropriately, the inspiration for the new design (the result of a comprehensive renovation that commenced in 1986), particularly in shapes, patterns and textures, is clearly Native American. However, the overall style in which this is executed is unmistakably Art Deco.

The original and fundamental idea of Art Deco was that an interior and its furnishings should form a complete design – 'a total look'. In this regard designer Candra Scott, a native of Oregon, has gone to impressive lengths. The attention to detail and the quality of execution are exceptional, and every individual feature contributes to an overall attempt to capture Oregon's history and spirit: the oak-leaf wallpaper in the bathrooms; the corridor wall lights, each a stylized bronze cast of a chief in a mica headdress; the old black-and-white portraits of Native Americans in traditional garb decorating the bedrooms; the beds inlaid with arrow motifs; the enormous mural dominating the lobby, by San Francisco artist Melinda Morley, which depicts the discoveries of Lewis and Clark; the lobby furniture, which mixes big leather homestead chairs with ceremonial drum occasional tables; and the lobby fireplace carved in the same image as the wall lights.

The design reminds me of the Musée National des Arts d'Afrique et d'Océanie in Paris.

The handmade lampshades feature
a pattern of stylized leaves
and early script

The imposing dimensions of the
Governor Hotel's interior suit
Portland and its history

With leather club chairs, Indian motifs,
and a roaring fire, the lobby has the
ambience of a ranch

The Governor Hotel's superb collection
of early twentieth-century photography
continues in the corridors

Poignant black-and-white portraits
of Native Americans appear
throughout the hotel

The cupola room at Jake's is
a reminder of the grandeur of this
late nineteenth-century building

The terrazzo floor and mural
decoration survive intact from
the late nineteenth century

The metal Deco face repeated in the
wall sconces and lobby fireplace was
found in a San Francisco antique shop

In the top floor of the new wing, the
Native American theme continues with
carpet, wall lamps and pendant lamps

Arrow-shaped marquetry inlay on the timber bedhead and portraits of chieftains continue the decorative theme

Included in the collection of predominantly Indian portraits is the odd cowboy

The mural that dominates the lobby depicts the discoveries of American pioneers Lewis and Clark

This carved head of a chief – a detail of the lobby fireplace – inspired the design of the wall sconces

Custom-made furniture such as this elegant porcelain lamp distinguishes the Governor's guest rooms

Lewis and Clark, first to chart the American Northwest, also encountered previously undiscovered tribes

Furnishings were inspired by research into the history of the Northwest and the international Arts and Crafts movement

Jake's, the Governor's restaurant, is one of the busiest and most popular in Portland

The food at Jake's is described as 'classic American grill cuisine' – specialities include 'cedar-planked' salmon

Dominated by vast murals illustrating the cultural contributions of Africa, and furniture and decorative detail inspired by African styles and icons, the Musée's 1931 interiors epitomize the harmonious relationship between furniture and surroundings that Art Deco sought to create. Substitute Native American culture for the folk art of the African tribe and you have the design of the Governor Hotel.

But what is it like to stay here? Suffice to say that, despite its magnificence, the design is only an added bonus. The main attraction is that the Governor is a people-magnet. Jake's, the hotel's bar and restaurant, must be the busiest place in town, and the Governor is *the* place for conferences and conventions (one look at the splendid period decor of the convention rooms explains why). In fact it is so busy at certain times that it seems that the residents of Portland can't get through a day without a visit.

The popularity of Jake's may well be due to the food, which is certainly well worth the wait for a table. Described as 'American grill cuisine', dishes include 'cedar-planked' salmon with Roma tomato basil wine and 'mahogany-glazed' chicken served on sesame-basted vegetables (all those timber references are very Northwest). But the ambience is as much of a magnet as the food, perhaps even more so. Jake's is like *Cheers* with a more stylish interior and a better menu.

The Governor Hotel is also not a bad place if you want to stay in. Room service is straight from Jake's and the rooms on the top floor of the west wing have cosy open fires (gas operated so you only have to press a button) for winter and large outdoor terraces with a view for summer. Even for fitness, the Governor Hotel is the place to be. Situated in the basement of the building is the Princeton Fitness Club, the biggest, best equipped, most comprehensive gym in Portland. Michael 'Air' Jordan and the Chicago Bulls were the last big names to train there…. And Nike? Aren't they based in Portland?

address The Governor Hotel, 611 Southwest 10th at Alder Street, Portland, OR 97205, USA
telephone (1) 503 224 34 00 **fax** (1) 503 241 21 22
room rates from US$185 (suites from US$200)

albergo del sole al pantheon

The Albergo del Sole al Pantheon is the oldest continually operating hotel in Rome. It also has the best location in Rome, directly overlooking the Pantheon, the most impressive of all the ancient remains in the city. This monumental temple, built by the Emperor Hadrian in the second century AD, and used as a Christian church since the early seventh century, has been depicted in countless sketches and drawings throughout Rome's history. Unlike so many other relics of ancient Rome that have fallen into disuse and become mere curiosities (the Forum was a cow field for much of the last century), the Pantheon continues to play an active role as one of the city's most spectacular and unusual churches. And its location, the Piazza della Rotonda, has been a popular meeting place since the Middle Ages.

A full tour of the interior of the Pantheon takes more than three hours. Its great size, particularly the towering height of the central dome, which rises some fifty metres from the ground, is almost impossible to reconcile with its age. Most extraordinary is the fact that it is open to the skies. When it rains, water enters through the apex of the dome and falls through the vaulted, gold-encrusted space onto a geometrically patterned marble floor, making

little puddles in the hollows worn by two millennia of foot traffic. Rome has countless magnificent remains, but none so captivating as this, still a place of worship just as it was when the Romans entered through its magnificent original bronze doors to worship their gods.

The Albergo del Sole shares something of the same sense of continuity and uninterrupted links to the remote past. The plaque on the fading sienna-coloured facade says this hotel has been an inn since 1467. Yet at first glance, on entering the hotel, all traces of this impressive heritage appear to have been obliterated. You certainly wouldn't guess that the hotel's guests have included the sixteenth-century poet Ludovico Ariosto and the eighteenth-century alchemist adventurer Count Cagliostro (who was arrested for hitting one of the inn's servants during his stay), or, more recently, Jean-Paul Sartre and Simone de Beauvoir. The interior is clean, simple and white, with terracotta tiled floors and a sparsely furnished lobby. The guest rooms are similar: white walls, terracotta floors, a magnificent antique bed, and very little else. It appears that only the facade has survived as evidence of the hotel's extraordinary pedigree. That is until you lie back in bed and gaze upwards.

Beautiful handpainted ceilings dating to the 1550s remain intact and provide a subtle but highly effective contrast with the unadorned simplicity of the rest of the hotel.

This typifies the Romans' relaxed attitude to their history, one of the main reasons why this is such an attractive city to visit. They live so much surrounded by antiquity that they don't concern themselves with trying to save everything. They simply isolate the elements that are important enough to keep and then proceed to live with and around them in a totally natural manner.

Food is the most important part of life here and always comes first. Even in a small inn such as the Albergo del Sole they have managed to salvage some space for a kitchen and dining area. Finding it is the hard part. Seven hundred years of changes, additions and renovations have resulted in a mini-labyrinth. There are staircases and doors everywhere and on two occasions, convinced that I had finally found the breakfast room, I charged straight into another guest room. Only by following the smell of fresh coffee (and some other guests who knew where they were going) did I find the hidden courtyard set aside for breakfast: a charming terrace, squeezed in among fading ochre-coloured buildings with ivy growing up the sides and creaky old wooden shutters.

Such unexpected little discoveries are what is so special about Rome. On every other corner, whichever way you walk, you can find delicious places to eat. The rules for avoiding a tourist trap are simple: open the door and listen. If you hear only Italian (the louder the better) ask for a table. First time out? Order the antipasto followed by pizza capricciosa. Romans are famous in Italy for taking time to enjoy their food (specialities include saltimbocca and lasagne), and there is an abundance of good places to eat. The fun is in seeking them out. This is not a city where you should find food with a guidebook. Just remember, if the place is full of Romans, the food will be good; if not, then keep looking.

address Albergo del Sole al Pantheon, Piazza della Rotonda 63, 00186 Rome, Italy

telephone (39) 6 678 04 41 **fax** (39) 6 994 06 89

room rates from L360,000 (suites from L600,000)

hotel eden

Rome has always been the ultimate tourist destination. Even during the Dark Ages no self-respecting Hun worth his Barbarian stripes could resist at least one proper sacking of this ancient city. And in the era of the Grand Tour, aristocratic young lords rampaging through the Tuscan countryside in the name of education and enlightenment would always save the best for last: Rome was the final destination, the cap to a one- or two-year voyage of discovery (and debauchery). Tourism and tourists are as much part of Rome as the Catholic church, and for the past hundred years, ever since the German couple Francesco and Berta Nistelweck opened the aptly named Eden, this hotel has been the top spot in one of the world's most visited cities. There is no shortage of names to be dropped. Ernest Hemingway, Orson Welles and Ingrid Bergman have all, at different times, made this Edwardian-era townhouse their home in Rome.

Of all of the eternal city's grand hotels this is the one to save your pennies for. The Eden is the glamour-girl of Rome hotels. Refined but not stuffy, sophisticated but not too grand, chic but not pretentious, it's glamorous in a *Roman Holiday*, Audrey Hepburn on the back of Gregory Peck's Vespa, kind of way. Hotel Eden is the very epitome of modern chic, with an unmistakable touch of Roman tradition.

First and foremost, there is the view. All of Rome is literally at your feet. From a commanding position on top of a tree-lined hillside, Hotel Eden looks over the Spanish Steps, Piazza Venezia, the Vatican and the River Tiber. No other hotel in the city can boast a panorama as sweeping and comprehensive as this. It takes in every site in old Rome that ever inspired a postcard. Situated just behind the Spanish Steps, Hotel Eden is less than three minutes on foot to Rome's most famous shopping streets. And judging by the number of guests hauling armloads of designer bags back up the hill to the hotel, that proximity is more than tempting. For those more inclined to sightseeing, all of Rome's most famous monuments are within easy walking distance.

Then there's the food. The rooftop restaurant, La Terrazza, with its breathtaking glass-enclosed view and its cosy outdoor terrace for lunch, could trade on its location alone. Add the Michelin-star cuisine of Enrico Derflingher, former chef to the Prince and Princess of Wales at Kensington Palace, and you have a combination that is proving hard to beat.

A gilded cherub is one of the few nods to the clichés of Roman design at Hotel Eden

The 100-square-metre terracotta-paved terrace of the presidential suite looks over the gardens of a neighbouring villa

A Roman touch: colourful stripes that recall the distinctive uniform of the Pope's Swiss Guard

The cuisine of chef Enrico Derflingher has earned La Terrazza a Michelin star

A spectacular Venetian mirror and a Doge's stool attest to Olga Polizzi's design team's eye for the finest pieces

The striking asymmetrical curtains are a single extravagant note amid a harmony of elegant restraint

A contemporary still-life at the entrance to La Terrazza sums up the relaxed, classically inspired interior

The rooftop location of La Terrazza gives the restaurant a view to match the spectacular food

Five stars without too much formality – the Eden is Rome's least pretentious grand hotel

Royal blue and a touch of gilding stand out like jewels in the Eden's gleaming off-white lobby

A handful of antiques in an environment of considered restraint is perfect in a city of classical antiquity

Trompe l'oeil murals decorate the walls of Tom Cruise and Nicole Kidman's favourite room

A plaque behind the glass door commemorates the hotel's reopening by Baroness Thatcher in 1994

The hotel bar has magnificent sweeping views of the seven hills of Rome

The lobby's polished terrazzo floor is a quintessentially Roman design ingredient

The outdoor terrace overlooking the gardens of Villa Medici is a perfect place for lunch alfresco

Very Roman in their lavish use of marble, fourth-floor bathrooms also have their own terraces

A typical corner room expresses the timeless but never clichéd classicism of Hotel Eden

Serving a menu described by Derflingher as 'mid-Mediterranean modern', this restaurant has become one of *the* places to eat in Rome. And it's always a good sign when, as here, locals outnumber guests in a hotel restaurant.

Closed for two years for a complete renovation, Hotel Eden reopened its doors in 1994. Designer Olga Polizzi, in collaboration with Richard Daniels, paid tribute to this city without ever lapsing into the obvious or clichéd. Surrounded by history and culture, the new Eden is appropriately classic and timeless. But thankfully there is not a Roman pillar or bust of Caesar in sight. In fact at first glance the elegant and tastefully furnished off-white lobby, with a judicious sprinkling of oil paintings and antiques, could be in Paris or London were it not for the distinctly Roman touches. The colourfully striped velvet cushions, for example, are a direct and witty reference to the famous striped uniforms of the Pope's Swiss Guard, believed to have been designed by Michelangelo. The immaculate

polished terrazzo floor is another ingredient true to its locale. Less obvious are the two bronze busts by English avant-garde ceramist Oriel Harwood that flank the entrance in a contemporary reference to the city's central legacy of classicism.

Throughout the hotel, dashes of brilliant colour and detail are set against plain, coloured walls, echoing, in a sense, the city itself, which is in part plain, simple and village-like, in part breathtakingly baroque. It wouldn't be Rome without a touch of extravagance, and at Hotel Eden this is contributed by the presidential suite. Decorated with trompe-l'oeil Etruscan murals, its true decadence is its voluminous terrace – an enormous expanse of terracotta paving that has proven particularly popular with Hollywood 'royalty'. In the days when Kenneth Branagh and Emma Thompson were a formidable duo, this was their Roman salon. Even Audrey Hepburn, after a hard day on the back of that scooter in her Givenchy shift, would have felt at home here.

address Hotel Eden, Via Ludovisi, 00187 Rome, Italy

telephone (39) 06 478 12 1 **fax** (39) 06 482 15 84

room rates from L550,000 (suites from L900,000)

hotel locarno

Small, intimate, stylish and highly individual, Hotel Locarno has consistently been voted the best three-star hotel in Rome ... and by Italian newspapers and magazines, no less. It is also a firm favourite with the film industry. In fact, with its Belle Epoque birdcage lift, crumbling terrazzo floor and genuine Art Nouveau bentwood furniture, it could be a film set. This is the kind of place where dark-haired women clad in clinging black and Manolo Blahnik mules arrive on the back of motorbikes and disappear into the lift, never to be seen again. With the outward appearance of a setting in an Agatha Christie novel, Hotel Locarno is a genuine enigma: though almost always full, you hardly ever see anyone, and when you do they almost inevitably slink away quietly at the slightest hint of someone else's arrival. It's one of the few places I've stayed where almost nobody turns up for breakfast. This is no place for early risers, nor for business meetings or power breakfasts.

The interior of the hotel reflects the fact that the owners, a mother-daughter team, have travelled extensively throughout Europe (and continue to do so) in search of antiques to furnish it. Over the years they have assembled quite a collection of Art Nouveau, Belle Epoque and Art Deco pieces, the periods they are most passionate about. In fact, the Locarno is really a never-ending design project for Maria Teresa Celli and her daughter Caterina Valente. The dining room, with its winter fireplace, features an impressive array of original Thonet bentwood furniture, as does the bar and the smaller winter breakfast room overlooking the courtyard garden. Even the windows facing the street were specially commissioned from an architect in the Nouveau style. They are so convincing that one would swear they have been there since the turn of the century. The hotel also has a sixth-floor roof garden with a commanding view over the River Tiber and the domes of the church tops in the Piazza del Popolo. During the summer months, which in Rome begin as early as March, breakfast is served on the roof terrace. It would be a perfect place to the start the day, if only some of the guests would wake up in time.

In a city with more than its fair share of tourism this is one of the few hotels that doesn't feel, look or act like a tourist trap. Considerable effort has clearly been put into this place, and the resulting ambience attracts a crowd that appreciates its individualism.

The bar and restaurant of Hotel Locarno
feature an extraordinary collection of
turn-of-the-century bentwood furniture

Old iron bedheads and antique tables
typify the individual design approach –
no two guest rooms are alike

A stone bird bath found by proprietor
Maria Teresa Celli is now the basin
in the restaurant bathroom

With a view of the street and courtyard, the Art Nouveau bar is popular for early morning espresso or late night grappa

The film noir atmosphere of the Locarno has made it a hang-out for artists, actors and photographers

The roof terrace with views over the church spires of Piazza del Popolo is the summer location for breakfast

It is also blessed with a great location, an added plus in a city where you should – indeed must – walk. How else could you stumble across one of those great little restaurants hidden in an alleyway and frequented only by locals? On foot (or perhaps on a Vespa) is the only way.

Hotel Locarno is just off Piazza del Popolo, the largest square in Rome, and located at the beginning of Via del Corso, so shopping is within easy striking distance. But first you may want to stop for a cappuccino, or a light lunch at Rosati, an elegant tea room and café overlooking the entire square. Piazza del Popolo is listed in almost every book about Rome as a great place to sit on the terrace of a café and do some serious people-watching. It's the perfect place to bask in the sun, watch the world go by and enjoy the luxury of being in the company of Romans as well as tourists.

Then there's the shopping. Walk and window shop along Via del Corso until you reach the Spanish Steps, whereupon you might want to head down Via Condotti for the bigger name label shops, such as Gucci, Prada and of course Rome's own, Valentino. Now that you are among the tourists you might as well give in and stop at Caffè Greco, a Rome institution for afternoon tea since the mid-eighteenth century, and still well worth a visit.

The message is clear: for people who make their own fun, who don't rely on hotels to pamper them and arrange everything, Hotel Locarno is the place. Popular with writers, photographers, film makers and musicians, it feels more like a film noir apartment building than a conventional hotel.

As *Vogue* points out, 'Rome's hotel trade has always been a lucrative one – with a steady captive market of cultural and religious pilgrims, most of the city's hoteliers have found it unnecessary to lavish money, care or imagination on their establishments. There are scores of seedy hotels occupying picturesque old convents, palaces and villas, but there are only a few small hotels of genuine charm and good quality.' Hotel Locarno is definitely one.

address Hotel Locarno, Via della Penna 22, 00186 Rome, Italy

telephone (39) 6 361 08 41 **fax** (39) 6 321 52 49

room rates from L250,000 (suites from L390,000)

hotel monaco

Hotel Monaco is unlike any other hotel in North America; but then San Francisco is unlike any other city in the United States. Ever since the gold rush of the mid-1800s San Francisco has been a hot destination. Just look at its profusion of hotels. Where else in the US have hotels specialized to the point of catering to specific professions and métiers? It has Hotel Rex for writers, for example, and the Phoenix for rock stars. It is not surprising then that this should be the city to give rise to an entirely new breed of hotel: the grand hotel with a twist.

Hotel Monaco has all the ingredients of a traditional grand hotel: the imposing marble staircase, towering ceilings, large fireplaces, plush furniture, armies of staff and prodigious luxury. And as in all grand hotels there's a famed dining room, a busy bar and a non-stop flow of people checking in and checking out, making dinner arrangements and going to the theatre – in short, a buzz of affluent activity. But at Hotel Monaco there is one thing distinctly missing – the stuffiness.

This is a grand hotel for a new generation. Because let's face it, most grand hotels are not really much fun. Sure, it's wonderful to be spoiled and pampered; its just the feeling that perhaps you should be taking up bridge that's

the worry. And all that quiet and hush-hush – how nerve racking! At Hotel Monaco the glamorous trappings of the grand hotel are packaged in an altogether more upbeat and youthful manner. This is not the relentlessly modern approach of Philippe Starck, designed to turn every convention on its head, but a more gentle twist of tradition. It would be a bit like Chanel Jr (if there were such a thing): twin set and pearls with younger legs and a shorter skirt.

Hotel Monaco is the flagship of the Kimpton Group, the hotel and restaurant empire founded by Bill Kimpton, a native of Kansas City. His philosophy is to combine food and design in a not too rarefied fashion. With hotels in Chicago, Seattle and Los Angeles, as well as half a dozen restaurants in San Francisco's Bay Area, it's obviously a formula that works.

Hotel Monaco's Grand Café is an established feature of the San Francisco scene. Located just one block from Union Square it makes a convenient inner-city rendezvous. There is a cosy familiarity to the bar that has taken it out of the 'latest and hottest' bracket and made it a regular hangout for locals – stylish, well-heeled locals, that is.

225

Dominated by modern art and sculpture, Hotel Monaco's bar is as busy as the restaurant

The decoration makes clever use of stripes and colour to create chic, cosy rooms

The Monaco's reception desk is styled to resemble a stack of old Louis Vuitton steamer trunk

A grand hotel for a new generation, the Monaco takes classic ingredients and updates them

The restaurant, in the tradition of the grand European brasserie, is also a popular meeting place for locals

The lively interplay of texture, colour and pattern gives the design of Hotel Monaco its fresh edge

The Grand Café is an excellent example of what makes Kimpton so successful. To begin with, it is really nothing like a hotel dining room. It is almost as if Kimpton started with a very popular restaurant, bar and brasserie and then decided to add a few rooms – I'm quite sure many people eat here without realizing there's a hotel attached. In sheer scale and opulence it offers a nod to the grand old hotels of the past, but in terms of food and ambience it is thoroughly contemporary, and stands on its own. And despite its capacious size the place is full every single day for breakfast, lunch and dinner – and not necessarily with hotel guests. In fact it has become such an institution that being a house guest does not necessarily guarantee you a table for dinner.

Much of the credit for this success must go to interior designer Cheryl Rowley and her distinctive 'tradition with a twist' approach. Her talent was particularly brought to the fore in the guest rooms. Colour, pattern and texture were all introduced to create a warm, funky atmosphere and successfully disguise the fact that the majority of rooms are a little on the small side. It doesn't matter. The array of stripes, cushions and cabinets is so welcoming that the proportions of the room only enhance the cosy comfort.

From the lobby desk – created from what at first glance appears to be a stack of old Louis Vuitton trunks – to the balloonists and clouds painted on the ceiling; from the profusion of pattern and colour to the elaborately styled chandeliers, age-old traditions have been reworked by introducing new ideas. Judging by the hotel's occupancy rates, it is an approach that is succeeding. Kimpton's signature combination of good food, good service and good design seems to be right on the money. His lesson in the realm of luxury hotels is clearly that to be different is just as important as to provide traditional standards of service and luxury. But not too different – just different enough.

---

address Hotel Monaco, 501 Geary Street, San Francisco, CAL 94102, USA

telephone (1) 415 292 01 00   **fax** (1) 405 292 01 11

room rates from US$199 (suites from US$409)

the phoenix

Squeezed in among the dirty brown buildings, massage parlours and X-rated movie houses of San Francisco's seedy (*Buzz* magazine prefers the word 'spicy') Tenderloin area, the Phoenix is definitely in the shabby end of town. First-time visitors, drawn by the hotel's rock and roll reputation, often arrive convinced the taxi-driver has made a mistake. But face it, if you want a hotel with some attitude, you're not going to find it in the chichi neighbourhoods.

The Phoenix is a hot favourite with the music world, and with all its press and media attention, as well as its dubious location, has earned itself quite a name as the bad boy of downtown 'Frisco hotels (a reputation that has only helped make it even more popular). There are plenty of stories about all the goings on at the Phoenix, and some are true – such as the time a reggae band threw all the plants in the pool – though most probably have less to do with truth than with selling newspapers. One fact, however, is undisputed. Rock stars like staying here. Just ask Sonic Youth, the Red Hot Chili Peppers, Radiohead, the Beastie Boys, Erasure, David Bowie, the Hoodoo Gurus, REM, Ziggy Marley, Sinead O'Connor, Debbie Harry or Tracy Chapman, to name but a few. And it's not hard to understand why. The area

is not too 'delicate' and the hotel has a big car park. Guests can make a lot of noise *and* their roadies won't have to worry about where to park the rig.

But the Phoenix is not just a hotel for bands who can't get in anywhere else. The roster of famous non-rock-star guests is almost embarrassingly respectable, including such unexpected names as John Kennedy Jr. So what's the big attraction? Very simply, the Phoenix is cool. In appearance, it's your classic all-American motel, just like the ones in the movies (*Thelma and Louise* or *Pulp Fiction* come to mind). Only this motel happens to be smack bang in the middle of the city. Rescued in the late eighties by hotel entrepreneur Chip Conley (who also created Hotel Rex) from its previous status as an hourly stopover for hookers and from the possible fate of the wrecking ball, it has every appearance of being a textbook American motor lodge. But it's not. Hiding behind a salmon-pink and turquoise fifties facade pretending to be a plain all-American motel is a carefully considered, art-filled environment. Like Andy Warhol's soup cans or Roy Lichtenstein's cartoon paintings, it's a familiar American icon remade to convey a new message.

With the addition of an enormous mural by New York artist Francis Forlenza, which covers an entire wall of an adjoining building, as well as some 250 other pieces of contemporary art that were introduced throughout the hotel, something completely new was created from something so familiar. Do the guests get it? Anthony Kiedis, lead singer of the Red Hot Chili Peppers, certainly appears to. He describes the Phoenix as 'the most sexually, intellectually and culturally stimulating hotel in San Francisco'.

Yet during the day the Phoenix is dead. In fact you would never know that the hotel was full. But that's just because everyone is still asleep. Only at night does the Phoenix, true to its name, start to come back to life. And once it does, the hotel bar and restaurant, Backflip, is the place to be. Designed in the style of a late-fifties Las Vegas cocktail bar, Backflip is like a permanent poolside party. With exotic private cabanas, a mirror-tiled fireplace, blue plastic banquettes, plastic fifties furniture and a bank of spot-lit fountains, Backflip permanently has the energy levels and high-octane atmosphere of a record launch. It's impossibly busy, impossibly trendy and impossibly difficult to get in. As a hotel guest, however, you not only have the benefit of assured entry but also the distinct convenience of only having to stagger across the courtyard to get to your room at the end of the night.

And what about the rooms? There are forty-four of them, each decorated in 'tropical bungalow style'. And, appropriately, they all look out over the 35-foot elliptical painted pool entitled 'My Fifteen Minutes – Tumbling Waves'. The rooms combine a collection of paintings by up-and-coming artists with tropicana kitsch – imported bamboo furniture, eye-height bird-of-paradise plants, and a palette of bright island colours that create a warm, inviting atmosphere that guests seem to grow fond of rather quickly. Even so, as they say, 'if you can remember your room, you probably didn't stay at the Phoenix'.

address The Phoenix Hotel, 601 Eddy Street, San Francisco, CA 94109, USA

telephone (1) 415 776 13 80 or (1) 800 248 94 66 **fax** (1) 415 885 31 09

room rates from US$109 (suites from US$149)

hotel rex

Hotel Rex has the ambience of a literary haunt. Although newly opened, this hotel feels like the setting of a thirties American film. It's the kind of place Bogey or Robert Mitchum would have felt comfortable, with a moody, mysterious feel just right for a rugged detective in a raincoat. It's a reminder of a type of hotel that hasn't been seen since John Huston's *The Maltese Falcon.*

The Rex has real atmosphere. It feels like a hotel for writers, and that is exactly what was intended. Acquired in September 1996 by the Joie de Vivre group, a specialist San Francisco-based small hotel group which also owns and operates the Phoenix and the Commodore Hotel, the former Orchard Hotel was completely redesigned with the aim of turning it into a West Coast recreation of the 1920s Algonquin, the legendary haunt of Dorothy Parker and New York's fast-moving, high-living literary set.

References to literature dominate the interior design. There is a small lobby bar, but no separate restaurant. Instead there is a library complete with leather-bound first editions and yards of solid mahogany cabinets, shelving and panelling. Surrounded by books, this is where guests are served breakfast in the morning, literary lunches are held during the day and people gather for drinks in the evening. The cosy but sophisticated bookish atmosphere of this ground-floor meeting place is enhanced by an impressive collection of thirties Californian art, handpainted lamp shades and big, comfortable, monogrammed club chairs.

The literary theme continues in the corridors with quotes from Dashiell Hammett and John Steinbeck decorating the walls, while the lift doors feature a collage of pages from the social registrars of the interwar period. In a radical departure from the pretty-pretty bedrooms of most small hotels, the rooms at the Rex are bold, simple and very masculine. A dark maroon carpet with royal blue and yellow stripes is combined with dark polished timber pieces and bedspreads in checks of green and white. And for the larger rooms, the furniture and ambience are once again bookish.

Prime location is a key aspect of the Rex's appeal. It is situated on Sutter Street, known for its galleries and antique shops, while Union Square, Chinatown and all of San Francisco's most glamorous shops and restaurants are only a short stroll from the front door. The central business district is also within easy walking distance, and the hotel offers a fully serviced dining room for special functions and conferences.

Hotel Rex has quickly made a name on the SF arts scene. It's the host hotel for the San Francisco International Film Festival and the planned venue for a series of literary launches. Howard Junker, editor of *ZYZZYVA*, a San Francisco literary magazine, shares the enthusiasm: 'it's a beautiful place and we're excited about doing readings, a salon or lunches there'. Kenneth Howe, writer for the *Chronicle*, sums it up when he says that the Rex 'goes big on ambience'.

Anyone familiar with the other hotels owned by the Joie de Vivre group, such as the Phoenix (also a Hip Hotel), will recognize Chip Conley's distinctive and idiosyncratic approach to the hotel business. Joie de Vivre's founding proprietor has thrived with a small hotel development formula that is all about targeting a niche within a niche. The Rex is for writers and the Phoenix is for rockers – or, perhaps rather more accurately, the Rex is for writers, bibliophiles and would-be writers, while the Phoenix is for people who are in, or would love to be in, the music industry. This projection of our wishes and desires is certainly not a new discovery in marketing. The fashion industry, for one, has been doing it for years. But Conley is among the first to apply the approach to the marketing of small hotels.

Yet anyone who instinctively cringes at the thought of a themed hotel should not be put off. This is theme, not theme park; Hotel Rex is most definitely not 'à la Disney'. Designers Ted Boerner and Candra Scott (who also created the interior of Portland's Governor Hotel) have resorted to nothing more tricky than old books, old paintings and big old club chairs to evoke an atmosphere unanimously (and surprisingly romantically) described in the American media as an authentic 'literary lair'.

address Hotel Rex, 562 Sutter Street, San Francisco, CAL 94102, USA

telephone (1) 415 433 44 34 or (1) 800 433 44 34 **fax** (1) 415 433 36 95

room rates from US$145 (suites from US$575)

regents court

It's easy to forget that Sydney is a city of five million people. Seduced by the surf beaches, enchanted by one of the most picturesque harbours in the world, blinded by the bright southern hemisphere light, anyone could be forgiven for mistaking this city for a resort. But Sydney is a new kind of metropolis; a city that, like Miami and Barcelona, is both convincingly urban and unashamedly hedonistic. Consistently voted by the readers of US *Travel and Leisure* magazine as the most desirable city destination in the world, Sydney is a sun-drenched capital with a sophisticated café culture. Regents Court, a small, stylish, inner-city hotel, is part of this culture: the perfect place if you're after some of the city's best cafés, bars and restaurants. For food (and Sydneysiders take good food very seriously) there is no better location in Australia.

Gastronomically speaking, Australia's English heritage is history. Thirty years ago the average restaurant menu still featured such anomalies (for a semi-tropical climate) as roast beef and Yorkshire pudding, but today it's more likely to be Sydney rock oysters and lightly seared South Australian blue fin tuna. Australia now has its own multicultural cuisine, based on the Mediterranean preference for fresh fish,

roasted vegetables and olive oil, but with the added and distinctive twist of Thai, Indonesian and Vietnamese spices, a reflection of its proximity to Asia. Above all else, Australian food is distinguished by the unsurpassed quality of its raw ingredients – a distinct benefit of life in a sparsely populated land of plenty.

'Foodies' should not therefore be disappointed that Regents Court doesn't have a restaurant of its own. It doesn't need one. Surrounded by some of Sydney's best restaurants, the hotel would only be depriving guests of culinary adventures. What it does have is a spectacular roof garden that runs almost the entire length of the building. In the shade of potted olive trees, surrounded by buddleia, orchids, oleander, agapanthus, ficus, white hydrangeas and frangipani, guests keen to experiment for themselves with the exotic raw ingredients of Sydney's famed fish markets are welcome to 'fire up the barbie' and do their own version of chargrilled Balmain bugs (a local crustacean that looks like it came off the set of *Lost in Space*). With city views to one side and a view of the Opera House and Harbour Bridge on the other, the roof terrace is the very typically Sydney space set aside for Regents Court guests to hang out.

In fact the terrace was the only space left: the rest of this 1920s gentlemen's tenement was already devoted to the rooms. Furnished in a combination of rich deep colours (chocolate brown, midnight blue), luxurious tapestry fabrics, dyed damasks and an enviable array of modern furniture classics by designers such as Mies van der Rohe, Harry Bertoia, Marcel Breuer, Verner Panton, Josef Hoffmann, Eileen Gray, and Charles and Ray Eames, the rooms look more like the apartment of a stylish architect than a hotel suite. Dating from 1990, the design has proven to be years ahead of its time. Cool, dark and handsome, the rooms represent the kind of low-slung, sexy, modernist aesthetic now promoted by Gucci – exactly the kind of pad that all the lifestyle magazines are currently hankering for. In keeping with the sophisticated design of the area's surrounding restaurants and bars, the architect and his partners at D4 design group resisted the more obvious lure of 'beach shack simplicity' and opted for 'pared-down inner-city' cool.

'The family', as a result, spent all their money on the furniture. The family are the MacMahons – as is often the case with Hip Hotels, Regents Court is a family affair. Tom MacMahon and his wife Paula run the show; Bill MacMahon, his brother, was the architect; and family matriarch Betty MacMahon, assisted by her sister Enid, is the roof-top gardener and contributor of the delicious home-made jams and tea-cakes that are served with breakfast.

The beneficiary of all this familial solidarity is definitely the guest. Staying at Regents Court feels like staying with a well-connected Sydney family that offer you their architect son's apartment for the duration of your stay (without having to make the bed) and allow you to entertain your own friends on their luxurious roof garden (without having to wash the dishes). No wonder this chic little hotel, despite being Sydney's best-kept secret, has become the hot favourite of artists, opera singers and other international *bons vivants*.

---

address Regents Court, 18 Springfield Avenue, Potts Point, Sydney 2011, Australia

telephone (61) 2 9358 15 33   **fax** (61) 2 9358 18 33

room rates from AS$165

das triest

In a city heavy with history, Das Triest is a light interlude. City of dancing horses, cosy cafés, *Sacher Torte* and Mozart, Vienna is steeped in history like few others. And unlike their Italian neighbours, the Austrians do not have the temperament to toss aside the baggage of history with a nonchalant shrug. In true eastern European fashion, heritage is taken as a weighty, serious affair. As former seat of the Hapsburg dynasty, this city, on the border of eastern and western Europe, has played a significant role in just about every event that has shaped the modern world. From its defeat of the all-conquering Ottoman Turks – knocking on the city's gates in the sixteenth and seventeenth centuries – to its pivotal role in the eruption of World War I, Vienna has seen and done it all. And it shows. There's scarcely a corner, square, park or avenue that is not adorned with a commemorative statue, bust, fountain or sculpture.

That's what makes this hotel such a welcome addition to Vienna. Das Triest is light and easy going – quite a contrast in a city where traditional Tyrolean costume (the kind worn by the entire von Trapp family in *The Sound of Music*) is still displayed in the window of every other 'fashion' shop. Das Triest is

a chance to throw that burdensome mantle of history onto a designer chair in the corner.

This hotel is an indirect result of the fall of the Iron Curtain. A decade ago, Vienna was suddenly no longer positioned on the outer fringe of a handful of repressed and politically estranged nations. Instead, it was the first and most conveniently located western city for its recently liberated eastern neighbours. With the collapse of Communism, Vienna emerged as a newly fashioned 'Hapsburg hub', springboard to the rapidly emerging markets of Hungary, Slovakia, Poland and the Czech Republic. It was in this dynamic climate that Dr Alexander Maculan identified a major gap in the Viennese market: the need for a hotel catering to a taste for civilized chic. If Vienna was going to make a serious bid to establish itself as the creative centre of eastern Europe, then it must attract art directors, ad agencies, photographers, stylists and so on – and if so, then it better have somewhere for them to stay.

The partners at first struggled to pinpoint the right approach for the hotel's interior: the proposals were all either too stark or too fussy. Until, that is, they were having dinner one night in Quaglino's in London. There they were inspired by Terence Conran's massive space.

The fireplace in the salon of Das Triest
is particularly inviting during
the cold Viennese winter

Overlooking the courtyard, the hotel
restaurant serves a modern version
of traditional Austrian dishes

The bar, a popular after-work meeting
place, has the leather-upholstered
intimacy of a private railway carriage

White bedlinen and cherry wood furniture define the warm but unmistakably modern rooms

The concierge desk in the black and white entrance – a classic example of Terence Conran's design

A beautifully sculptural staircase leads from the lobby to each of the hotel's seven floors

They immediately decided to invite Conran to Vienna to do the same with their property. He gave them just the look they wanted – modern but not hard. With warm cherry wood and furniture upholstered in bright shades of blue, red, yellow and green, he created a sense of comfort that offsets the acres of white walls.

Not that Das Triest has turned its back on history. Built in the mid-seventeenth century just outside the city gates, it was a hostelry during Austria's imperial reign, accommodating the footmen and horses of the royal mail coach en route to Austria's only seaport, Trieste (hence the hotel's name). The salon retains the original vaulted ceilings of the royal stables. Divided into separate areas by gilded folding screens, the various vaulted conversation spaces of the lobby offer intimacy and privacy. And the restaurant, a long rectangular space with a view of the courtyard garden, has done with the food what the building has done with the architecture, serving a lighter, less self-conscious version of Viennese tradition.

The tribute to Vienna's glorious history continues with the black-and-white prints throughout the hotel by Viennese photographer Christine de Grancy. Her photos capture the city's spectacular array of busts and statues from a roof-top perspective: an appropriate introduction to Vienna's architectural triumphs. And given its location, Das Triest is a great place from which to take in the real thing. The view from the top-floor terrace offers a panorama of the city's monuments, most spectacularly the brightly coloured mosaic roof of St Stephen's, the Gothic cathedral.

When you weary of the spectacle of Vienna's treasures, there is always the spectacle of the scene in the hotel. At night Das Triest really comes alive. Here one can see the truth of Ian Schrager's claim that 'hotels are the nightclubs of the nineties'. All of Vienna seems to hang out here, spilling out from the bar into the lobby and restaurant in a ritual that comes close to a nightly full-blown party. As a guest you never need be on the outside looking in.

---

address Das Triest, Wiedner Hauptstrasse 12, A–1040 Vienna, Austria

telephone (43) 1 589 18 0   **fax** (43) 1 589 18 18

room rates from 2,100 AS (suites from 6,400 AS)

widder hotel

Just off the famous Bahnhofstrasse in the very heart of old Zurich there is a picturesque little side street called the Rennweg. It is packed with boutiques and restaurants and delicious little pastry and chocolate shops, just like Swiss streets are supposed to be. It is only after walking straight past yet another seventeenth-century picture-postcard shop front that you realize you've just missed the entrance to Zurich's most celebrated new hotel, the Widder.

This is definitely *not* what you would expect from a five-star hotel located in the centre of a major city, especially a Swiss city. But then the Widder is unlike any other hotel. It's not just the entrance that is disguised on this charming shopping street: the entire hotel is completely hidden within a complex of houses dating back as far as the eleventh and twelfth centuries. From the street it is difficult to discern the presence of any hotel at all.

In all, Widder Hotel comprises ten different historic houses, beginning on the Rennweg and bending around the corner into the Augustinerstrasse. Originally owned separately by feudal guilds, the properties were purchased collectively by the Union Bank of Switzerland in 1970 as an investment. Faced with a property of paramount historical sensitivity,

a special preservation committee was established which eventually selected Tilla Theuss as the architect who would convert the properties collectively into a modern hotel. And what a task! A bigger bureaucratic hurdle is hard to imagine. Not every member of the city council thought this project was such a great idea (no surprise) and the job got even harder when initial work uncovered priceless sixteenth-century frescoes, rare river-stone floors, precious painted ceilings and an original city wall dating from the twelfth century. Not only did each new archaeological discovery have to be incorporated into the overall scheme, but work slowed to a crawl in fear of damaging some other as-yet-undiscovered remnant. Add to this the fact that the ten houses had somehow to be united as a single unit without altering the individual structure of each and it's hardly surprising that this ambitious project ended up taking more than ten years in planning and construction.

In the end, Theuss allowed the history and experience of each individual house to determine the design. The Augustiner House, for example, is decorated in Biedermeier fashion, while the interior of the Pferch House is seventeenth-century Baroque, and so on.

A room in the Biedermeier style in the Augustiner House, one of ten individual houses comprising Widder Hotel

Rustic hand-painted local antiques are combined with modern classics throughout the hotel

The mezzanine of this seemingly modern, loft-like space is an unexpected find in a seventeenth-century building

Ornate painted murals were uncovered by accident during the early stages of the construction work

Eames chairs, a modern fireplace, a mosaic terrazzo floor and original river-stone walls define the lobby bar

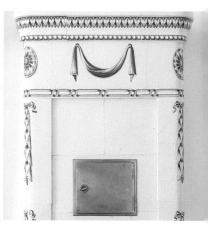

The Biedermeier ceramic stove was one of many historic treasures saved during the renovation of these old city houses

In summer, the outdoor terrace adjoining the lobby is a pleasant surprise in the heart of old Zurich

An original sixteenth-century mural contrasts with the modern furniture of the Augustiner House

Situated on a quaint shopping street in the historic city centre, it's impossible tell from the outside that this is a ho

The painted beams of the Widder's private dining room are sixteenth-century originals

Breakfast is served in the high-tech atrium, whose cantilevered glass roof opens in the summer

Some of the fragments of wall murals date back as far as the thirteenth century

The duplex rooms of the Pfeife House are uncompromising in their modernity

Even the Widder's meeting rooms feature the results of the hotel's ten-year renovation

The dark panelling and sombre tones of the furniture are in keeping with the style of the Pferch House

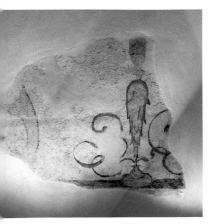

Renovation work progressed slowly because of the chance of uncovering fragments of historic frescoes

Tucked into the basement is the Widder Bar, one of Zurich's hottest jazz clubs

The view from the terrace of the Widderzunft House, with Lake Zurich in the background

The result is a bewildering variety of architectural and decorative styles which, coupled with the complexity of links joining the ten different houses, has created a veritable design labyrinth. Every corridor and staircase leads to yet another unexpected room or space, in yet another architectural style and mood. And there are corridors and staircases everywhere. The intricacy of the overall structure makes it easy to lose your way. Even after studying the plan closely, I couldn't work it out. But I like it that way. The whole notion of hidden places and spaces evokes childhood memories of playing in the attic – the fun is in *not* knowing what you'll find. Anyone who relishes the unexpected and abhors predictability will definitely love it here.

So too will the design aficionado. This hotel is a furniture lover's paradise. Every famous piece of modern furniture by the biggest names in design and architecture is here – somewhere. Le Corbusier, Mies van der Rohe, Adolf Loos, Charles and Ray Eames, Eileen Gray, Josef Hoffmann, Frank Lloyd Wright, Mario Bellini, Harry Bertoia … the list goes on. This feast of modern classics is distributed throughout the hotel, helping to bridge the hundreds of years of different history and heritage it encompasses.

Needless to say, each and every one of Widder Hotel's forty-nine rooms and seven suites is completely different. In an ideal world, as a guest, you would select the fantasy and style that appeals most. In reality, Widder Hotel is far too popular for you to be able to do this, so the policy is good old-fashioned pot luck. But this works surprisingly well, challenging guests to experience environments that often challenge and change their preconceived opinions.

For the reader concerned at what may sound like very 'un-Swiss' randomness, complexity and unpredictability … do not fret! Widder Hotel has earned its five stars the hard way, by providing standards of service that are typically Swiss – i.e. immaculate.

---

address Widder Hotel, Rennweg 7, CH–8001 Zurich, Switzerland

telephone (41) 1 224 25 26 **fax** (41) 1 224 24 24

room rates from 370 SFr (suites from 780 SFr)

British Library Cataloguing-in-Publication Data
A catalogue record for this book is available from
the British Library

ISBN 0-500-28111-4

Designed by Maggi Smith

Printed and bound in Singapore by C.S. Graphics

Acknowledgments
Photography by Herbert Ypma, with the exception of
the Sukhothai; the Peninsula; Blakes; the Hempel;
the Prince of Wales; Regents Court; and Widder
Hotel, all generously supplied by the hotels.